T0114856

Latex Concrete Habitat

A manual on construction of roofs for recovery from world poverty

by

Dr. Albert Knott
Dr. George Nez

ISBN 1-4120-3997-5

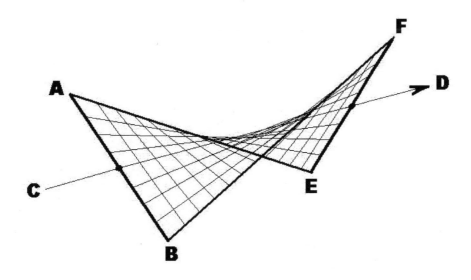

Order this book online at www.trafford.com
or email orders@trafford.com

Most Trafford titles are also available at major online book retailers.

© Copyright 2005 Dr. Albert Knott and Dr. George Nez.

All rights reserved. No part of this publication may be reproduced, stored in a retrieval system, or transmitted, in any form or by any means, electronic, mechanical, photocopying, recording, or otherwise, without the written prior permission of the author.

Print information available on the last page.

ISBN: 978-1-4120-3997-0 (sc)

Because of the dynamic nature of the Internet, any web addresses or links contained in this book may have changed since publication and may no longer be valid. The views expressed in this work are solely those of the author and do not necessarily reflect the views of the publisher, and the publisher hereby disclaims any responsibility for them.

Any people depicted in stock imagery provided by Getty Images are models, and such images are being used for illustrative purposes only.
Certain stock imagery © Getty Images.

Trafford rev. 09/13/2018

Trafford PUBLISHING   www.trafford.com

North America & international
toll-free: 1 888 232 4444 (USA & Canada)
fax: 812 355 4082

Index to Latex Concrete Habitat

Appendices

Latex Concrete Roofs Being Built by Dr. George Nez on Preexisting Walls for a School in Wardak Afghanistan

Chapter A

Latex Concrete Roofs for Resettlement and Refugee Camp Conditions

Thin shell latex concrete shell roofs are one answer to low cost construction of immediate shelter of displaced people groups.   Latex liquid and Portland cement are generally available in any region that has a paint and construction industry.   The materials are readily available in India, China, Iraq, Central America, and in the southwestern regions of the United States, regions where poverty and the need for housing abound.

This booklet describes this form of construction, and is presented as a contribution to the conversation on recovery from world poverty. It presents a simple form of roof construction capable of being built by unskilled labor. Materials and mix proportions can vary to match local availability.

The Concept of a Latex Concrete Roof Structure

The Edge Members: Take four poles, two 10-0" feet long (3.1 m), and two 10'-9" long (3.3 m), and bind them, or fasten them together to form a rectangle with the two longer poles meeting at one corner. Lift that corner and prop it up on a post sticking 4 feet (1.2 m) out of the ground. The frame will now be 10 feet square in plan. Miter the four corners to make adjacent ends fit snugly together.

The Screen Surface: Mark off the two lower poles in ten 12-inch lengths (31 cm) by shooting staples into the wood as guide marks. Mark off the two upper (longer) poles in 10 segments, each segment being 13 inches (33 cm) between staples.   Stretch 1-foot wide strips of fiberglass fly-screen from one side of the frame to the other in both directions, layering them on, lapping the strips approximately 6-inches with the one below, and stapling the strips down using the guide marks as alignment references. Note that each strip will fan out from the one below due to the larger guide mark spacing on the upper poles. Start installing the fly-screen from the low sides first, placing a single staple in the middle of each sheet at each end, then pulling the four corners of the sheet tight to complete the alignment. Then staple each of the four corners in place. Wrap the fiberglass fabric around the poles and staple on the back side. Continue adding stripes left and right in a herringbone pattern until the surface is covered. The fiberglass screen will form a curved surface when finished called a *hyperbolic paraboloid*, or HP surface. Any gaps or "fishmouths" can be eliminated by shifting the screen, or sewing the upper and lower layers together through the screen. Due to over-lapping, the finished surface will be four layers of screen in thickness.

Coating the Surface: Coat this surface first with a mixture of latex liquid and Portland cement (latex slurry) applied using long handled brushes. The latex slurry should be about the consistency of wet paste. The latex liquid can be cut with water on about a 1 to 1 ratio to make the cement slurry. Brush the surface both from above and below during the application to guarantee that all of the layers are wetted through. The wetted surface will harden relatively rapidly, so work with small batches of the slurry.

Now add a soupy mixture of latex slurry and sand (latex mortar) until the surface has been built up to about $3/_8$-inch thick (1 centimeter). The ratio of dry sand to Portland cement can be about 3 to 1. This surface, when it air-cures and hardens, can be walked on. Be certain to parge the fabric all around the edge members to cause good adherence. About midway through the parging process, the edge attachment can be strengthened by stretching a 3-foot wide strip of flyscreen lengthwise along each pole, wrapping the layers around each pole, and stapling it in place into the pole, and into the newly parged fabric, both from above and below. This will assist the latex concrete surface in transferring future loading to the edge members. This surface construction is what the writer's refer to as "latex concrete."

A simple model was built by Albert Knott to illustrate this technique of construction. See the *HP Shell with Tie*, shown below. The model was made by threading four soda straws onto a string, tying the string together to form a four sided rectangle, propping one corner up, then adding Scotch tape in a laced pattern to form the surface.

The single shell described above can be tilted and propped up as shown in the photograph. Buttress the lower opposite corners of the shell or tie them together across the span to keep the corners from spreading under gravity loading. The tie can be made from twisted and parged fiberglass fabric parged onto the shell with latex concrete.

Latex Concrete (LC) Surfaces Have Many Uses.

The above model shell is supported at three points. It could be supported on two, three or four. These LC membranes can be built to form HP roofs, arched shelters, and walls, and in any strength desired when built up by adding additional layers of fabric and mortar. It can be perforated for smoke stacks and sky lights. It can be used to build water tank floors, walls and covers. It can be used to make large sewage treatment tanks and small rain diversion gutters. Latex slurry can be mixed with soil and compacted by tamping to make insect proof, durable floors. It can be mixed into scarified soil and tamped to form basins for catching rain water for drinking and irrigation purposes, or for replenishing underground aquifers in arid climates.

HP shell model using soda straws and Scotch tape.

Buttress or tie between supports to prevent shell spread under load.

HP Shell With Tie

Study Model for an HP Shell Roof by Albert Knott

The material can be used to make water buckets, grain baskets, ropes, and buried and above ground tension ties. The latex material can be simply left over latex-based house paint. It can be sludge from a latex batch plant cut with water. It can be obtained from most manufacturers in 55 gallon drums and 5 gallon pails. It can be obtained in powdered form for ease of light weight shipping.

And the resulting construction can be built using unskilled labor.

A New Replacement for Old Roof Construction

Historic house construction in many third world countries involves heavy exterior stone, brick, or mud walls, coupled with heavy tile, or wattle and mud roofs. The mud roofs are supported on poles or small beams which sag, causing ponding and seepage of the roofs, and the use of timber for roof joists uses up precious fire wood. This old form of construction is heavy, inefficient, maintenance intensive, and consumptive of natural resources.

The latex concrete surfaces are light weight, and strong. They carry their loads in membrane compression and tension. Bending is eliminated. Cathedral roofs span long distances because they carry their considerable weight in arch compression. The Denver International Airport Terminal Building tent roof structure spans long distances because it carries its greatly reduced weight by in-plane skin tension. Concrete shell structures carry their loads in tension and compression in their skins, hence do not need to be heavy and thick as is required in historic roof construction. The historic roofs carry their loads not in shell action, but in massive bending.

Resettlement Villages

In resettlement situations where total re-roofing of a town is needed for housing, for community buildings, for shops and markets, these light, wide-spanning HP roof modules in varying sizes up to 15 feet square can cover entire buildings or court yards. They are particularly suitable in housing emergencies at community scale, in refugee encampments or in areas vulnerable to high winds, floods or earthquakes. In comparison to conventional roofing, these thin-shell concrete roofs offer many significant advantages.

For example:

- Lowest total cost for roof materials and labor,
- The shells can be rapidly built,
- The thin-shell roof is stronger and more durable than conventional construction,
- The roofs require little or no maintenance,
- Maintenance and repair do not require special tools or procedures,

- With lateral bracing, the shells can be set up on their own supporting posts, thus entirely relieving wall loading and allowing any local wall materials to be used,

- Given initial technical assistance and hands-on experience with demonstration units, this roof construction can be built entirely by local labor, family groups, and volunteers,

- Only hand tools are required,

- No production factories are needed. No large equipment is required. No formwork is needed,

- Electricity is not essential, but a small generator can double production by allowing night work,

- Roof modules can be assembled on the ground without scaffolding, and later lifted into place by hand,

- For larger modules, light boom trucks or fork lifts can make short work of moving and hoisting the roof sections,

- With this readily-learned roofing process it is possible to make quick use of existing repairable walls,

- Construction can start immediately without waiting for wall construction.

Roofs First:

To maximize the efficiency of construction in resettlement areas, the roofs can be built and erected *first*, then can be left in place by the construction teams. This is called *"Roofs-First Construction."* When a roof is in place, families will naturally move in under the roof, and go to work themselves building the walls and interior spaces. Refugee camps, and populations displaced by natural disasters have idle labor readily available to work on housing.

Too often, delays in disaster recovery come from trying to rebuild housing in traditional ways. Traditional materials and methods in most war-torn or re-settlement areas call first for rebuilding the heavy bearing walls, because the walls are necessary to carry the traditional heavy tile or earthen roofs. The builders of tile roofs often can not get the tile. The tile factories may be no longer available. Thus, reconstruction comes to a stop. The *"Roofs First"* technique using these light weight shell roofs allows early recovery for displaced populations. A community project of people helping each other heightens morale, and hastens recovery.

Four Segment Shell on Any Combination of Walls

Four of these 10-foot square roof elements can be joined together along their upper or ridge beams to make an extended assembly 20 feet on a side. The four single shells are joined by tying adjacent ridge beams together, and applying fiberglass fabric over the joining lines, brushing on more latex mortar to make the structural connection contiguous and watertight.

A four-shell assembly can be positioned over any combination of pre-existing walls if a supporting framework is built into the shell frame construction at ceiling level. As shown in the photo below, a four-shell framework can be built with four (or eight) edge beams, only four ridge beams, and an integral tie beam frame lying horizontally in the plane of the ceiling.

Four Segment Roof of Latex Concrete on Preexisting Walls

Model by George Nez

An advantage in ease of hand erection of larger shells and shell assemblies can be achieved if only one coat of the latex slurry is applied to the four shells while the framework is still on the ground, the other heavier layers of latex concrete being applied after the assembly has been moved up onto its final supports.

While still on the ground, the first coat of parging is applied. The single frame with its four integral shells is then raised into the air by lifting the roof assembly using pallets and jacks. The frame is then moved laterally onto the walls, then is anchored in place. Then the remaining coats of parging are applied.

Summary

Latex shells get their strength from their shape, hence are light weight, and portable. They are the lowest cost in materials of any form of construction due to the fact that very little material is used. They are buildable by un-skilled labor with minimal training.

Latex shells are permanent, versatile, and require little maintenance. Their use can eliminate the long construction time, the heavy materials weight, and the drain on natural resources characteristic of reconstruction of most historic indigenous architecture.

Latex concrete roofs are ideal for refugee camps, and for resettlement and recovery from natural disasters. If a ceiling is built into the construction as shown in the model, thermal insulation can be added to control the tempera-ture swings characteristic of construction in arid regions.

Chapter B

Vaulted Latex Concrete Shelters

Vaulted shelters are habitats wherein the structural ribs meet and are bound together over head. Please refer to the Barrel Arch in Photograph No. 1. This vaulted shelter is made by embedding flexible poles or tied willow bundles in the ground in two parallel trenches, and pulling the tops down until they can be bound together at the tops of the poles or willow bundles coming up from the opposite side.

Photograph No. 1 – Barrel Arch Shelter

Model by George Nez

The bottom four feet of the poles or willow bundles are wrapped in fiberglass fabric and heavily parged with latex slurry[1] to waterproof and strengthen them. Then they are positioned in 3-foot deep parallel trenches

---

[1] Latex slurry is a mixture of latex liquid and Portland cement mixed to the consistency of paste.

in the ground, adjusted so that they all exit the trenches at the same slope, and permanent, interior, longitudinal tie beams are tied in place at ground level at the base of the arch ribs (not seen in the photograph), and at above head height on the interior walls to guarantee this alignment. Concrete is then placed in the trenches and vibrated or tamped to permanently encase the pole ends. A day or more should be allowed for curing of the trench concrete before arch tying.

The top ends of the poles are then pulled down until they cross in the middle, and a permanent ridge beam is added. Then the tag ends of the poles are pulled on down, the geometry is adjusted to guarantee a smooth arched shell, and the tag ends are bound tightly to the opposing poles, completing each arch. Permanent cross ties across the shell, as shown in the photograph, can be placed after the longitudinal poles have been secured and the tag ends have been bound in place.

The low rise barrel arch shown In Photograph No. 2 is similar in construction, but with the poles laying over more in the trenches prior to concreting. The low rise arch has the advantage of easier access to the top and underside of the roof during construction, but has the disadvantage of reduced usable floor space.

Prior to application of the latex concrete surfacing[2], the ribs should be wrapped in fiberglass fabric for their entire length, and painted with the latex slurry coat. This will allow bonding of the shell surface to the ribs when the final surface is added, will increase shell flexural strength in resistance to wind loading, and will enhance resistance of the structural ribs to insect attach.

The fiberglass fabric can be laid in any width due to the shape of the arch, each strip being overlapped to the one before by 6 to 12 inches. The fiberglass can be laid horizontally, and vertically across the shell (and stapled to the base beam and the ribs), the first layer running horizontal to span between the ribs, and the last running vertical to enable ease of brooming in final latex concrete placement, or they can be laid diagonally in a herring bone pattern. Start with the bottom layers of herring bone, and work upward across the arch. Care should be exercised to eliminate gaps and fish

---

[2] Latex concrete is a broomed on mixture of 3-parts <u>dry</u> sand to 1-part Portland cement with enough latex liquid added to obtain a workable mix. Recommended ratio of latex <u>solids</u> to cement is 12 to 18 percent by weight. Recommended ratio of water to cement is 35 to 38 percent by weight. Note that latex liquid is normally latex solids <u>plus water</u> in approximately a 50-50 ratio by weight.

Photograph No. 2 – Low Rise Barrel Arch Shelter

Model by George Nez

mouths. Sewing through the fabric to make it lie flat may be necessary in places, prior to parging.

Native yurts and hogans can be painted directly with latex slurry with or without fiberglass, then painted with latex concrete to obtain a durable, although non-movable, habitat.

A third example of arched rib construction is the circularly symmetrical ribbed dome shell shown in Photograph No. 3 below. This shell shape has the advantage that it echoes many types of indigenous architecture, hence may be more readily acceptable to a native culture. However, it has the disadvantage of awkward placement of the fiberglass fabric. It will be necessary to use shorter runs of the fiberglass fabric and more narrow widths, and it may be appropriate to try to staple and slurry paint each sheet as it is initially placed so that the next sheet can be glued in place to achieve the needed curvature.

Photograph No. 3 – Ribbed Arch Dome Shelter

Model by George Nez

Chapter C

Construction of a 20' x 20' LC HP Roof

A hyperbolic paraboloidal surface, or HP surface, is a saddle shaped surface formed when a straight line translates laterally, and rotates at the same time about an axis lying along its direction of travel.   As in Figure 1, line AB translates along the axis CD and rotates about CD to reach position EF.   The surface ABFEA is an HP surface.

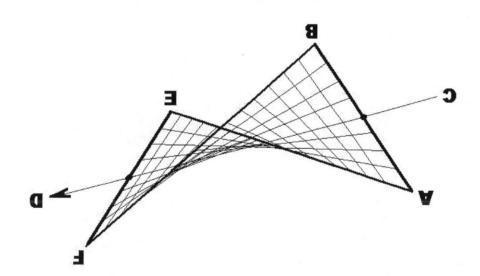

Figure 1 - Hyperbolic Paraboloid Surface

Such a surface can be approximated by taking four soda straws of equal or varying lengths, and threading them on a string, then tying the string together to make the soda straws form a quadrilateral. Lift one or more corners of the quadrilateral up onto a prop to make a shape that looks like Figure 1. If I now mark each edge beam off into an equal number of segments, and take Scotch tape and attach strips of the tape to the soda straws making each strip cross the opposing guide mark on the opposite edge member, then when I get the surface all filled in, I will have formed a curved HP surface.

When working with such HP shells, it is a good idea to build several models of your proposed structure out of soda straws and Scotch tape to work out the desired geometry. Do I want the corner propped up more, or less? Do I want the sides to be equal to each other, or unequal? If I make the soda straws different lengths, what different shapes will be formed? The writers have used this technique to explore not only geometry, but also habitability. How will a person, or a family use the proposed shelter? If I join several HP shapes together, can I cover a larger area? What will be the overall geometry of the finished structure?

The roof structure shown earlier and repeated in Photo No. 2 below is a four quadrant HP shell roof formed by joining four HP shapes together along the ridge lines. The model shows two segments roofed, and two segments open. Inside you see an area which can be used as an attic. The living spaces below can be a variety of sizes and wall locations as the shell is framed to edge members and ceiling joist members lying in a horizontal plane to allow for any orientation of supporting wall below. The roof model is shown separated from the walls below in Photo. No. 3.

Photo No. 2 – Four Segment HP Shell Roof on Existing Walls

Model by George Nez

An LC HP shell is an HP shell made of latex concrete. Latex concrete is fiberglass fabric stretched over a large frame as was the Scotch tape in miniature above, and the resulting fabric surface is then saturated with first a slurry of latex and Portland cement (a liquid paste), then when that dries, a $^1/_4$ to $^3/_8$ inch thick layer (or layers) of latex concrete made of latex liquid, Portland cement, and sand is broomed on. The latex concrete is typically made by mixing Portland cement with dry sand to a 1 to 3 ratio by weight, then adding latex liquid until you get a broomable mix.

Photo No. 3 – Another view of the Same Four Segment Model

Purpose of this Chapter

In this chapter, the writers will describe the construction of a four segment LC HP shell for eventual use as a residential roof. The example roof will be 20 feet by 20 feet in plan, constructed on the ground using dimensional lumber, then lifted into place and supported on four columns. Walls can be built later. The model in the photograph above shows a series of ceiling beams bearing on the walls and carrying the shell roof. The proposed 20-foot square frame will have edge and ridge members only, and be supported on four columns as shown in Figure 2 below. The columns will be positioned at the midpoints of the sides, attached to the connection where each of the ridge and edge members join, and the connections at the tops of the columns will be tied together across the shell with tension ties to carry the lateral thrust of the ridge beams.

Four columns set in the ground will carry the frame. The four column bases will be waterproofed by wrapping the column bases tightly in latex concrete and founding them in post holes backfilled with concrete.

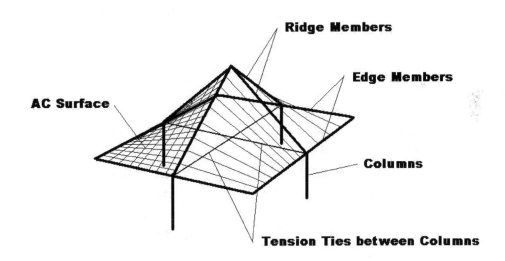

Figure 2 - The Frame

Each segmental shell will be 10 feet square in plan to cover one quadrant of the 20 foot by 20 foot roof. If the ridge members have a 4 in 12 slope (arbitrary) the rise will be 3 feet 4 inches in 10 feet. The peak of the roof will be 3'-4" above the plane of the roof line.

The length of the ridge members will be

$$L = \sqrt{(10^2 + 3.33^2)} = 10.54 \text{ feet} = 10'\text{-} 6".$$

Each ridge member will be a T in cross section with a 2x6 horizontal head, and a 2x6 vertical stem glued and nailed together. See Figure 3-A below. Each edge member will be an upside down U consisting of a 2x8 head piece 10 feet long, oriented horizontally, a 2x4 by 10 feet long vertically oriented outside piece with the head piece glued and nailed downward onto it, see Figure 3-B, and finally a 2x6 inside piece 12 feet long, centered over the support post, oriented with the long face vertical, then glued and nailed to each head piece of the adjacent edge members. See Figure 3-C on the next page. The columns will be 6x6 square timbers, or 6-inch diameter round posts. After bolting the inner 2x6 to the column top, the space between the column and the outer 2x4 will be filled with latex slurry grout, packed, and then the outer 2x4 will be bolted to the column top through the slurry.

Framing the Edge Members

The four shells will be built on a frame of edge members 20-foot x 20-foot in plan. This frame is first built on the ground, and will later be raised into position on top of the columns.

The overall length of the 2x8 head plates of the edge members is 10 feet even. Glue and nail the 2x8 head member and the 2x4 side member together. Miter the ends of the edge members which make up the four corners of the 20 x 20 frame at 45 degrees so that they will fit tightly against each other in the final assembly. Then lay them in pairs upside down on the ground so that the under surface of the 2x8's are showing. Now, glue and nail in place 20-inch x 20-inch x ½-inch plywood gussets in each of the mitered corners to fix the angle of the edge members at 90 degrees to each other. See Figure 4 for the upside down gusset plate.

After installation of the four corner gussets, the four edge member frames can be turned back over, and joined by installing the 2x6 inside plates as shown in Figure 3-C.

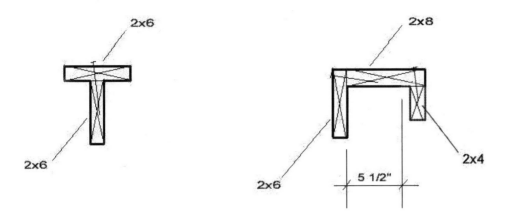

Figure 3-A
Section at Ridge Beam

Figure 3-B
Section at Edge Beam

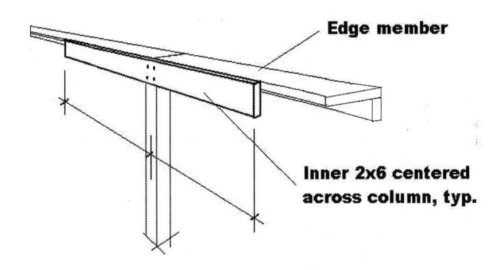

Figure 3-C   View of Condition Over Posts, Typical 4 places.

Figure 5   Crown Block Geometry

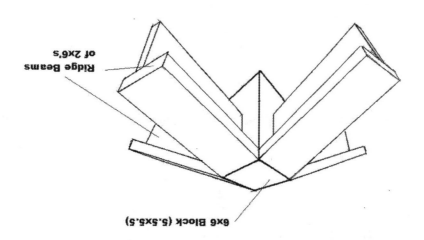

Ridge Beams of 2x6's

6x6 Block (5.5x5.5)

The 2x6's that make up the ridge members must frame together at the top, and must be cut to fit for uniform bearing. Cutting-to-fit when the four ridge members are sloping up toward the crown at a 4 in 12 slope is geometrically awkward. Therefore, it is recommended that the four members frame into a short piece of 6x6 column oriented vertically, called a *crown block*. See Figure 5. All sloping members can now be cut at a uniform 4-in-12 slope to fit against the vertical faces of the block.

The Framing of the Ridge Members at the Crown

Figure 4 - Gussets Under Edge Member Corners

Upside down edge members with mitered corners

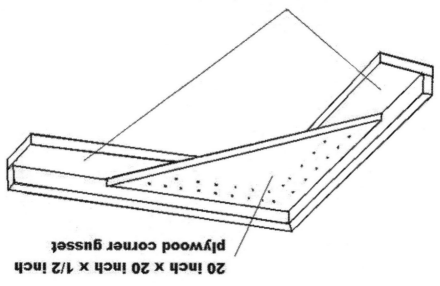

20 inch x 20 inch x 1/2 inch plywood corner gusset

This framing can be easily accomplished by laying two ridge beams on their sides on the ground, cutting the ends to be joined at 4-in-12 slopes and fitting them against the crown block also laying on its side on the ground. The joint can be nailed together, and the resulting frame can be tilted back upright and fitted to the edge member frame. The installation of the other two ridge beams to the crown block can be accomplished by simply leaning the ridge beams into place and nailing them.

Framing of the Lower Ends of the Ridge Beams onto the Edge Members.

The cutting of the lower ends of the ridge beams to fit the edge members is more complicated, and requires careful measuring and sawing. The detail is shown in Figure 6 below. Dimensions are in inches.

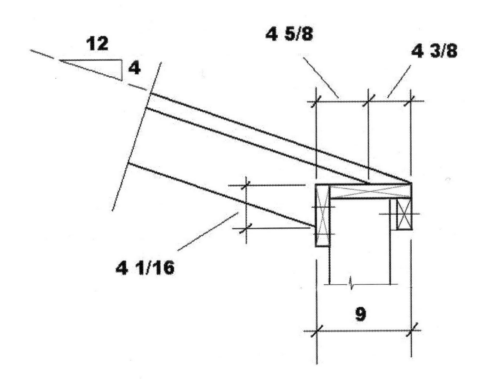

Figure 6 – Ridge Beam to Edge Beam Connection Geometry

The ridge members can now be mounted on the edge member frame with the ridge members centered over the butt joints of the edge members and the crown block centered at the top. When in place, and aligned, bolt the edge members to the column top using four 5/8-inch diameter by 6 inch long lag screws, with washers, equally spaced in predrilled holes. Also bolt the 2x4 edge members to the column using 5/8-inch by 6-inch long lag screws with washers. Bolt through the 1/2-inch space between the edge members and the column, and pack the space tight with latex concrete to close.

Column Spread Under Load

The gravity loads carried by the roof are delivered to the edge and ridge members by in-plane shear in the latex concrete surface of the roof. Thus the edge members push against each other over the columns (hence a well fitting butt joint is required), and the ridge beams push downward and outward on the tops of the columns. This outward thrust delivered by each ridge member pushes outward on the tops of the columns and needs to be resisted to keep the roof from spreading and trying to flattening out.

This resistance can be accomplished in a variety of ways.

1. The top of each column can be tied across the building to the top of the opposite column using tension ties,
2. The tops of the columns can be braced back into the soil to carry the thrust into the ground, or
3. The foundations and columns can be made strong enough to allow the columns to carry the load in outward column bending.

The total weight of the loaded 20-foot by 20-foot roof for a quarter-inch of latex concrete plus a 30 pound per square foot snow load is approximately:

W = The dead weight of the roof + the live load of snow.

Dead weight = $4 \times [(10+10.5) / 2]^2 [1/4''] [140 \text{ pcf} / 12]$ = **1240 pounds**

Snow load = $20 \times 20 \times 30 \text{ psf}$ = **12000 pounds.**

W = $1240 + 12000$ = **13240 pounds**

As shown earlier, the length of the ridge member in a 4-in-12 sloping roof will be:

L = $[3.33^2 + 10^2]^{1/2}$ = **10.54 feet.**

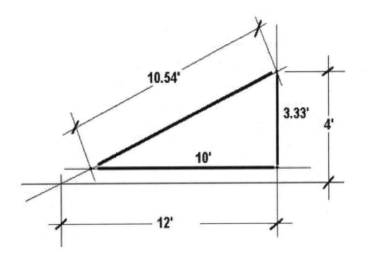

Figure 7A   Dimensions of a 4-in-12 Slope

This total roof weight of 13240 pounds is resisted by the four ridge members of length 10.54 feet pushing upward on a 4-in-12 slope.   In accordance with Figure 7B the axial load in the ridge member necessary to do this is:

R = ¼ [10.54' x 13240 / 3.33'] = 10,477 pounds per ridge member

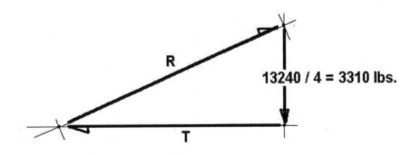

Figure 7B   Force Diagram for Ridge Beam and Tension Tie

The outward thrust of the ridge member is the horizontal component of **R**, which is:

T = ¼ [10/3.33] x 13240 = 9940 pounds per ridge member.

These are fair sized structural loads and should not be ignored[3]. They can not be ignored in larger hypars or shells with a lower height. It would take a ¾-inch diameter steel rod to carry the load in this 20'x20'x3.33' HP shell. The rods can be threaded each end and for steel nuts, and inserted through holes drilled through the columns within a foot of the tops of the columns. The nuts should bear on 5" x 5" x 3/8" steel bearing plates on the outside faces of the columns. After the shells are in place the nuts should be tightened sufficiently to take the sag out of the rods.

Note: These forces will decrease in magnitude as the height of the crown increases. For example, an increase in height of the crown from 3'-4" to 4'-0" will change the tie rod tension from 9940 to 8275 pounds, a decrease of 17 percent.

Applying the Fiberglass Fabric to a Quadrant of the Frame

Mark the length of the two horizontal edge members in 12 inch intervals by using a stapler gun. The ridge beams should be marked in 12-5/8 inch intervals, starting from the bottom of the ridge beam (the outer edge of the edge member) as they are somewhat longer than the edge members. This will give an equal number of intervals marked on each member. These stable marks will be guides for placement of the fabric.

Cut eight runs of fabric 3 feet wide and 12 feet long. These will be the final covers for covering the edge and ridge members of the frame with fiberglass. Cut the remaining fiberglass fabric into runs of fabric 12-inches wide by 12 feet long.

Starting at a lower edge member, stretch a 12-inch wide run of fabric parallel to and in line with the inside surface of the outer lower edge of the 2x4 of the edge member. Staple this to lie flat and up the slope of the surface. See Figure 8. Run a second line of 12-inch wide fabric perpendicular to the first along the edge of the adjacent edge member, stapling it also to lie to flat.

Using a run of fabric 12-inches wide, staple the center of the fabric to the top surface of the ridge beam using a single staple, and aligning the edge of the fabric with the bottom edge of the 2x8 of the edge member. Staple the lower edge of this run to the lower edge member with a single staple in the center of the run of fabric, again aligning the lower edge of the fabric with

---
[3] They can be ignored by omitting the ties, but shell warpage and undue edge member stress will result.

the lower edge of the 2x8. Then pull the four corners of the fabric tight from each end to obtain a smooth alignment, and stable the fabric down in its four corners. The fabric should lie smooth and flat and begin to form the slope of the shell surface.

Next take another 12-inch wide run of fabric, overlapping the one below by approximately 6 inches (half its width), and using the guide staples in the frame members to ensure alignment. Do this in successive opposing directions left and right in a herring bone pattern, working up the slope of the surface, placing 3 staples in each end of each run of fabric until the surface of the shell is entirely covered. The surface will be four layers of fabric thick when finished, and all layers should be lying straight and smooth without gaps or fish mouths.

The tag ends of the 12-inch wide runs of fabric at the ridge members can be left loose, hanging over the edge of the ridge top plate to be plastered to the underside of the next shell surface when the latex slurry is later applied. See Figure 9-A below.

When finished with all four frames of the roof shell, run 3-foot wide strips of fabric up the ridge members, centered on the ridge , and along the edge members to encapsulate the tag ends. This will strengthen the fabric on the four sides of each shell surface.

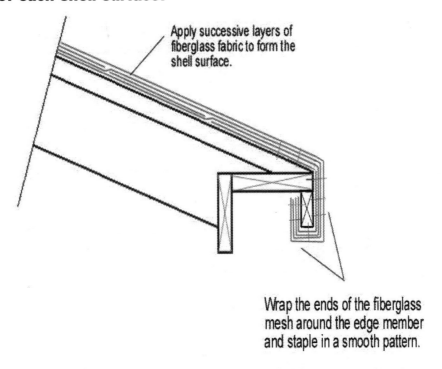

Apply successive layers of fiberglass fabric to form the shell surface.

Wrap the ends of the fiberglass mesh around the edge member and staple in a smooth pattern.

Figure 8 – Wrapping Fabric at the Edge Beam During Application

The Slurry Coat (SC)

The slurry coat, used as a first coat on fiberglass surfaces, is a paste of la-tex liquid and Portland cement. Viscosity of the slurry coat can be con-

Figure 9-B Screen Is Then Parged Down During Slurry Coat Application

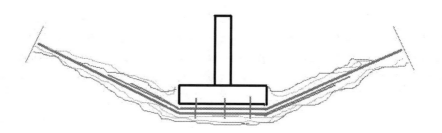

During the application of the first latex slurry coating, these tag ends of the fiberglass fabric are incorporated in the slurry and glued to the shell surface from both above and below. See Figure 9-B.

The strips of fabric were applied in runs parallel to the edge and ridge mem-bers, alternately overlapping, and stapled. At the ridge beam the staples were driven into the upper surface of the 2x6 plates. As shown in the sketch 9-A the tag ends of the strips were allowed to extend beyond the far edge of the ridge beams and hang freely.

Figure 9-A Fiberglass Screen is Lapped Across Ridge Beam During Application and left hanging.

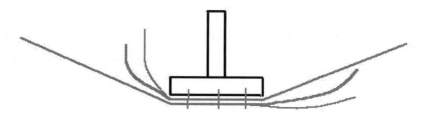

Condition of the Fabric at the Ridge Beam

trolled by adding fine sand. The slurry is painted or brushed onto the fabric, and put on thick enough to work down through the fabric layers. The application from above should cause slurry to extrude out through the fabric on the under side of the shell where it can be worked back up into the layers of fabric by brushing. The frame can be lifted several feet and set on pallets to allow workers to brush the slurry into both the upper and lower sides of the surface. Thoroughly coating the shell surface from both sides guarantees that the fibers of the fiberglass will be fully incorporated and work as a whole to carry load. After painting with the slurry, allow the surface to dry and harden before continuing. The additional heavy coatings of latex concrete materials (latex slurry with gap graded sand added) will be applied later.

Latex Liquid Materials

Latex liquids are a mixture of polymer latex solids suspended in water. They have the appearance of milk. Manufacturers of the basic materials typically supply the latex material at a mix of about 50 percent solids to 50 percent water by weight. This material is then used by manufactures of construction liquids such as latex paints and cement additives by adding additional water, coloring, and special chemicals such as antifoaming agents. Some trade-named materials are Laticrete, Rhoplex E-330, Rhoplex MC-76, Rhoplex MC 1834 emulsions, and Acryloid MC-46, a solid grade latex resin powder. They all have properties in common. They improve mechanical strength and adhesion properties, and impart the ability of the concrete to air cure. They remain stable in Portland cement, and resist the penetration of water, hence provide concrete with good freeze-thaw resistance, and low moisture penetration. They can readily bond with themselves. Latex paints are typically at about 20 percent solids by weight. The Rhoplex materials listed above are sold at about 47 percent solids.

The strength of latex concrete is affected by excess water in the mix. For that reason it is best to work with dry sand. It is to be noted that the specification given above *of "3 parts sand to 1 part cement, then add latex liquid until you get a workable mix"* is a *craftsman's* type of specification. If you are working with sand which already has a moisture content of 7 percent, then you do not need to add the latex milk to get a workable mix. Therefore, if you add the latex to wet sand, you will be watering down what latex you have, and not getting the advantageous physical properties you want in the finished product. Use dry sand.

Latex Concrete Specification

If the percent solids information is available from the manufacturer of the latex materials you are using, try for a ratio of polymer _solids_ to cement by weight of 0.12 to 0.15, and a water to cement ratio by weight of 0.35 to 0.38.

Wrapping the Column Bases

Eventually, the shell will be lifted into the air higher than it will finally be, the columns will be placed in pre-excavated holes, the column bases will be wrapped with latex concrete then the holes will be packed with concrete, the shell roof will be lowered into position and attached to the columns, and the column ties will be installed. Therefore, the column holes and the column bases should be prepared in advance of frame construction.

The proposed column is a 6x6 timber, or a 6-inch (or larger) diameter pole. If it is desired to have the bottom surface of the shell edge beams at 7 feet above the ground, the columns should be cut to, say, 10 feet long to fit into 3-foot (or more) deep holes. Rocks or concrete can be placed in the bottom of the hole upon which the columns can bear during erection. The rocks or shims can allow adjustment of final column height.

The timber base of the column can rot in the ground. To minimize this form of deterioration, the base (the bottom 4 feet) of the column should be wrapped tightly in fiberglass fabric, and heavily parged with latex slurry to seal it. The parging should come up the column to at least 12 inches above the final grade of the surrounding soil.

Thus, the column holes are dug, the column bases is waterproofed, the columns are fitted into the holes and adjusted for height, then the columns are laid aside to await their final placement.

The Latex Concrete Coat (LCC)

When the columns are finished, the latex concrete coat (LCC) can be applied to the shell surface. The LCC is a mixture of latex slurry with sand added to increase its thickness, weight, stiffness, and water resistance. Mix dry sand and cement in a rotary mixer (or in a trough) to a 3 to 1 ratio by weight, Add latex liquid as needed to make a workable mix. As the LCC will harden relatively rapidly during application, mix only as much in each batch as can be placed in a few minutes to allow a uniform layer of LCC to be applied to the shell surface prior to the mortar taking a set. To apply a surface that will eventually be 3/8-inch thick, apply layers of say 1/8-inch thickness, working around the shell. This will require going over the shell surface several times.

The LCC should be poured or thrown onto the surface, and the materials should be spread downward with a brush or broom. Applying it high on the shell and letting it run down the surface as it is broomed into place is appropriate.

To facilitate placing the mortar high on the shell, the top several layers of fabric can be left off producing an opening at the crown of the shell from which a worker inside on a ladder can pour fresh LCC to flow down the surface. This opening can be later closed, and the final fiberglass layers can be parged while walking on the hardened shell surface. See the sketch on the front cover of this manual.

Problems

Problems can occur during the application of latex concrete. The lower reaches of the surface may begin to sag as the weight of the wet LCC comes onto the fabric. These lower four corners may sag so much as to allow water to pond during the later service life of the shell as a roof. To prevent this early sag, the fiberglass fabric can be propped up before or during the LCC application to prevent ponding pockets from forming. Placement of plywood panels in the four corners before LCC application, and propping them up off of the ground is practical. Packing the space above the corner triangular gussets with LCC prior to final shell application is practical. Making the height of the shell greater in the middle during the preliminary design is a good solution.

Final Trimming

The final step in finishing the roof surface is to finish tying down the tag ends of the fiberglass membrane at the edge beams in accordance with Figure 8 and 9, stapling, trimming and parging with slurry coat and LCC to provide a finished workmanlike appearance. This is important because this wrap-around trimming provides the grip that the shell surface has on the edge member, and is necessary for full shell structural integrity. It is important that the initial slurry coat be heavily applied at the ridge and edge members so that it thoroughly wets and bonds to the wood surfaces below.

Lifting the Shell, and Column Placement

After the LCC surface has been allowed to dry for a few days, the shell can be lifted into its final position. The four corners were earlier placed on stacked pallets to raise the shell into a position so that a person could brush the shell surface from below as the first slurry coat was applied. After the shell surface has dried, this lifting procedure can be continued, lifting or jacking up each corner in sequence and shimming the shell with additional pallets as it rises. Raise the shell by this procedure until the shell is approximately 8 feet off of the ground.

The columns can now be dropped into the foundation holes, moved into alignment, and braced in position. The columns should be aligned with the edge beam spaces above, then the shell can be lowered into place by removing pallet shims. Position the columns to fit within the edge beam pockets as shown in Figure 3-C above. Brace the roof into position by guy lines and lateral struts to prevent any movement in the event of wind or inclement weather. Anchor the shell to the column tops with 5/8-inch diameter by 6-inch long lag bolts with washers through the 2x beams into predrilled holes in the timber column head.

Backfill the foundation holes with concrete, or latex concrete, and tamp or vibrate the concrete so that it seeps into the spaces at the base of the hole, and fully encloses the entire column base. Slope the top surface of the foundation concrete to cause water to drain away from the column bases.

Install the steel tie rods between the column tops just below the 2x8's of the edge member, and tighten the nuts on the rods. Brace the roof and column structure in place for at least four days to allow the concrete to set up and the shell to dry cure. When the shell and foundation concrete is cured, the tie rods can be further tightened to eliminate rod sag. At this time the roof can be inspected for completeness, uniformity, and water tightness.

Chapter D

Selection of Materials

Basic Construction

In latex concrete construction, fiberglass screens are stretched two ways over a timber frame, then a latex slurry coat and one or more heavy sand/cement/latex coats are brushed or broomed on and cured to form a hardened membrane surface. Assembly techniques of these surfaces are given in several papers.[4,5,6] The purpose of this chapter is to present and discuss types of fiberglass screen and the latex materials used in this construction.

Fiberglass screen

The screen used in the shells is an open weave, meaning that there is substantial open space between the adjacent strands.[7] Such screens are typified by the common insect screen available from many building supply or hardware sales outlets. These screens have strands of the order of 0.01 inches in diameter that are woven in a 18 x 16 pattern, that is, there are 18 strands per linear inch of width of the screen, and 16 strands per linear inch of screen length. Other strand sizes and other strand densities are acceptable, so long as the openness of the screen is sufficient to permit a bonding agent to readily permeate the screen, but not so open as to adversely affect the closing of each opening by the bonding agent.

Fiberglass strand has a strength of 200,000 to 220,000 pounds per square inch of cross section of the glass strand.[8] The maximum elongation is very

---

[4] Knott, A.W. and Nez, G.: *Latex Concrete Roofs for Resettlement and Refugee Camp Conditions*, Proceedings, Engineers Without Borders Conference, Boulder, Colorado, Oct. 2003.

[5] Curtis, Evan H.: *The Fabrication of a Fiberglass Reinforced and Latex Modified Portland Cement Hypar*, U.S. National Park Service, Denver Service Center, Falls Church, VA, 1985.

[6] Knott, A.W., Nez, G., Keyes, C.: *Construction of a 20" x 20' AC HP Roof*, Proceedings, Engineers Without Borders Conference, Boulder, Colorado, Oct. 2003.

[7] Kersavage, J.A., United States Patent 3,927,496, December 23, 1975, U.S. Patent Office, Washington D.C.

[8] Curtis, Evan H.: *The Use of Fiberglass Scrim and Screen in Ferrocement and Thin Shell Concrete Structures,* U.S. National Park Service, Denver Service Center, Falls Church, VA, 1985.

small, thus glass fabrics neither stretch nor shrink appreciably. Other useful properties of fiberglass are that it is electrically nonconductive, it is not combustible, it is resistant to most chemical solutions (except alkaline, as in cement), and it is almost completely unaffected by fungus, bacteria, and insects.

Use of non-metallic screens in cement, other than fiberglass, is not considered prudent because under tension loads, these yarns stretch. Only screens made of metal or fiberglass should be considered for tension load-carrying elements.

A description of a fiberglass yarn would include the filament diameter, the number of filaments per strand, and the number of 100 yard lengths of yarn per pound of yarn. The weave of the screen would also be described as the number of yarn strands per inch and whether they are twisted or plied together.

"ECG 150 1/0" is an example of a specific yarn frequently used in fiberglass screen.[9] It uses E-glass ("E" for good electrical resistance) in a "C" or continuous filament of "G" size (9 micrometers or 0.00036 inches). The "150" means that one pound of the yarn has a length of 150x100 = 15,000 yards. The "150" value is also related to the number of "G" filaments in the yarn. The one in "1/0" means that this yarn has one single strand in the yarn. It may be twisted to hold the filaments together. The zero in "1/0" means that no twisted strands are plied together in the completed yarn. A 150 G yarn has about 200 filaments per strand. Screen manufacturers frequently call this an 11 mil yarn; but the 11 mil dimension also includes the pvc coating on the yarn. "ECG 100 1/0 yarn is used in a screen with a finished pvc coated yarn of 13 mill diameter, and this yarn has about 300 filaments per strand.

Another term encountered with fabrics and screens is "Denier." A denier is the weight in grams of a 9,000 meter length of the yarn. It is a unit of fineness. The smaller the denier value, the lighter the yarn. The "ECG 150 1/0" yarn would be a 300 denier yarn.

The strength of fiberglass can be chemically affected by the cement used in the concrete. The loss of composite durability and flexural strength occurs when the calcium hydroxide crystals in the hardened concrete have formed

---

[9] Curtis, Evan H., *The Use of Fiberglass Scrim and Screen in Ferrocement and Thin Shell Concrete Structures*, U.S. National Park Service, Denver Service Center, Falls Church, VA, 1985.

on or among the fibers of the fiberglass yarn bundle. Alkalinity of the cement attacks the commonly available E-glass type of fiberglass. The US Army requires that fiberglass be made of high-zirconium glass, (AR glass). AR-glass is "alkali resistant" glass. Williamson (1985)[10] explains that the theory regarding protective mechanisms associated with the addition of a water-disbursed polymer relates to the fact that the space between the fibers in a glass fiber bundle averages about 3 microns, whereas the smallest cement particles average about 30 microns in size. Therefore, space between the fibers does not fill with cementitious material. Eventually this space becomes filled with cement hydration products (e.g. calcium hydroxide) which, though not as hard as glass, are suspected of notching the fiber's surface when placed under load. If this happens, the glass, which is very notch sensitive, would lose considerable tensile strength. This in turn reduces the composite strength. However, when polymer is added to the mix, the particles being only 0.1 to 1.5 microns in diameter can fill the interstices between filaments in a glass fiber bundle. This not only prevents the formation of hydration products, but also provides a matrix between the fibers that is (1) soft enough to preclude mechanical degradation under load, (2) assists in the load transfer between fibers, and (3) helps protect the fibers from alkali attack. Tests indicate that these protected products retain sufficient strength that they qualify for use in cement composites to carry load. Use of AR-glass and polymer additives avoids a loss of durability.

To minimize the concern about glass degradation from alkalinity in cement, it is advisable for the designer to use AR-glass where possible. AR-glass stands for "alkali resistant" glass. However, AR-glass is not commonly available in a screen. The next best choice would be to use E-glass which has a pvc (polyvinylchloride) coating designed for use in cement. J.P. Steven & Co. manufactures a 9x9 fabric E-glass screen using ECG-075-1/0 yarn (10 pounds per yarn) and a 20x12 fabric screen using ECDE-100-1/0 yarn (6.5 pounds per yarn). The coating on these screens is designed for use in cement board. A pvc coated fiberglass screen coupled with the latex in the modified cement provides a stable arrangement.

The use of white screening with non-cementitious, liquid latex can produce a translucent surface permitting sunlight to be admitted into the interior of the structure.

---

[10] Williamson, Gilbert R. *Evaluation of Glass Fiber Reinforced Concrete Panels for Use in Military Construction,* Technical Report M-85/15, construction Engineering Research Laboratory, U.S. Army Corps of Engineers, Champaign, Illinois, 61820, June 1985.

Determining the Tensile Breaking Strength of Fiberglass

Breaking strengths of fiberglass fabrics range from 20 pounds per inch to 900 pounds per inch of fabric width, depending on the construction and the yarn content. The fiberglass screen proposed for use in a structure can be field tested to determine its tensile strength by use of the following procedure.

Ultimate Tensile Strength

1. Cut a 2 inch wide by several feet long strip of fiberglass from the length of a roll.
2. Select a horizontal section of a limb in a tree or an overhead beam and staple one end of the fiberglass to it, wrapping the strip around the limb.
3. Wrap this strip several times around the limb, and parge it to stiffen the fabric.
4. Wrap it several more times after the parging is dry so that the last several wraps of the fabric are not parged.
5. Wrap the other end of the strip symmetrically around a 12 inch length of 2x4 and staple and parge the first several wraps. Then wrap the strip several more times around the 2x4. Round the edges of the 2x4 before wrapping to eliminate potential cutting edges.
6. Finally, nail a 1x4 hanger frame to the ends of the 2x4 as shown in the Figure 1 drawing below.
7. Now, by hanging known weights to the hanger frame, the strip can be put into uniform tension until it fails.
8. The tensile strength is the weight the strip carries, divided by the width of the strip. If it fails at 450 pounds, then the strength of the 2-inch wide strip is 225 pounds per linear inch.
9. Test several such setups and select the least value obtained as a conservative estimate of the ultimate tensile strength of the fabric.

Creep Strength of Fiberglass

It will be noted that if you leave a weight hanging on the strip of material, that the strip may fail over night. This experiment should be performed at the load level chosen as the ultimate strength, and the strength estimate reduced if necessary.

A second concern exists about screen fabrics. Some fabrics are plastic screen, not fiberglass or metal. If you pour boiling water down the hanging specimen and the specimen stretches unduly, then it is plastic. Some fiberglass fabrics are glass coated with PVC or other soft material. Such fabrics also stretch as the glass fibers cut into the coating. Such fabrics should be avoided if possible as well, as long term sag will occur in the resulting roof structure.

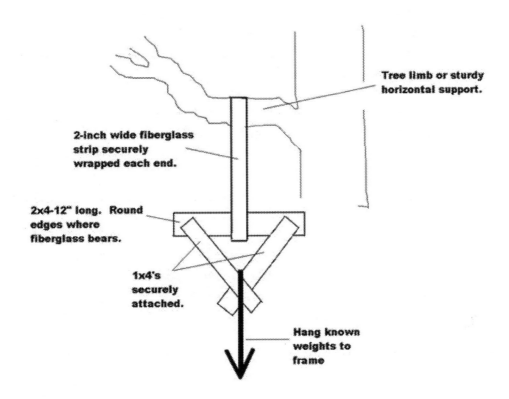

Figure 1 – Tension Test Configuration for Fiberglass Fabric

2-Way Fabric

A typical pvc coated fiberglass insect screen available at local stores is 18 x 16 fabric (18 warp yarns per inch by 16 fill yarns per inch). Similar screens are manufactured by a number of firms. Normal lap of 6-inches for 12-inch wide runs of screen laid both directions produces a surface which is four layers thick. Methods for calculating the necessary overlap of adjacent runs of screen based on required strength are available.[11] Overlaps often run

---

[11] Curtis, Evan H.: *A Method for the Design of a Low-Cost Fiberglass Reinforced Thin Shell Concrete Hypar*, U.S. National Park Service, Denver Service Center, Falls Church, VA, 1985

from 4 to 8 inches. Some designers overlap all fabrics half way due to the ease of layout, and ease of keeping the successive runs lying flat.

Because it is necessary for the finished screen to lie flat on the curved hy-par surface, it is an advantage for the designer to select narrower widths of screen because they can be installed with fewer "gills" or fabric separation areas.

The flyscreen roll is first sawed into uniform widths and each run of fabric is stretched between opposite edge members and stapled down.[12] The first run of screen is placed over one of the lower edge members, is stretched tight, and a single staple is placed in the center of each end of the run, and into the edge member. Then the four corners of the run are stretched tight, and the four corners are stapled down. Then a second run running perpen-dicular to the first is stretched and stapled over the second edge member. Then a third run is lapped six inches over the first run, stretched and sta-pled, then in the perpendicular direction the fourth run is stretched and sta-pled. This left-side-right-side sequence will produce the mat thickness of four layers when the surface is completed.

Starting with the first screens stapled to the edge members, then working up the slope means that adding a slurry to the surface will cause the plies to remain closed and not gap open as the concrete material is applied. The wet material tends to run down the surface, and the ply laps conveniently open downward.

For a shell which is square in plan with two edge members lying parallel to the ground, the two ridge members leading to the crown of the shell will be longer than the edge members. The length of the ridge members will be the square root of $(a^2 + h^2)$ where a is the length of the horizontal edge member, and h is the rise in the shell. The runs of the fabric will therefore fan out as the runs ascend toward the ridge beams. This spreading is called the *run advance of the screen.*

It is prudent to mark the edge beams in increments of the run advance for each run. A 10x10x4 foot shell can have a run advance of 12 inches at the edge beam if ten runs of 18-inch wide screen are going to be used with a 6 inch overlap per run. The edge beam can be marked with staples driven in at 12-inch centers. The ridge beams, being longer, can be marked in an

---

[12] Sawing the mesh can produce an airborne powder of glass fragments which could be harmful if inhaled. Wear a mask or tie a cloth over your mouth when sawing as a safety precaution.

equal number of increments as on the edge beams, but the marks will be in 12-5/8 inch increments on the ridge beams. Guide staples can be driven into the wood of the edge and ridge beams at these run advance intervals.

The ends of the fly screen strips are wrapped three quarters of the way around edge members and stapled with 3 to 6 3/8-inch staples per end in a workmanlike manner. After completion of the laying of the fiberglass fabric, and the application of the first slurry coats, a three foot wide run of fly screen can be laid over the edges and stapled down to provide a smoothly layered perimeter laminate. This edge strengthening ply will reinforce the region most susceptible to early failure of the shell surface. Finally a small nailer strip can be run up the inside of each frame member to nail down the tag ends of the flyscreen in under the edges of the shell.

Care should be taken that not too many layers of screen are put down before parging with the slurry coat, as they may prevent the movement of the slurry coat through the fabric, and out on the far side of the screen. The slurry coat should fully encapsulate all layers of the screen, and minimize voids. The extrusion of the slurry coat through to the opposite side of the shell should be observed, and brushed out to fill the screen openings. It may be practical to stop during the screen placement process and apply slurry coat at intermediate levels, or to make a special effort to force the slurry coat through the multiple layers of fabric.

How Many Layers of Fabric Do We Need?

Assume that we had done the testing for strength of the fiberglass fabric by suspending the test frame in a tree, and the 2-inch strip of fabric had failed at 60, 66 and 74 pounds for the three specimens we tested. Assume that we had poured boiling water down the fabric and 2-feet of the fabric only stretched about a quarter of an inch. Therefore, we decided that the strength of the fabric we would use was 60 pounds, the least of the test results, and dividing that by the 2-inch width of the fabric, we concluded that we could plan on the fabric demonstrating an ultimate strength of 30 pounds per inch of width. Therefore, our 12-inch wide strip in Figure 2 should carry 30 x 12 = 360 pounds per linear foot of width, per layer of fabric, for loading applied parallel to the run of the fabric.

But, our fabric will be laid in runs parallel to the edge beams, not running up and down the arch length **AB**. Therefore, the component of the force in the fabric in the direction of the parabolic arch will be 4 layers at 360 pounds x cos 45° = 1018 pounds. Therefore, we have a capacity to carry 1018 pounds in the 12 inch wide surface **AB**, and the applied load, T_A, is 650 pounds.

Factor of Safety

An applied load of 650 pounds on a fabric the working strength of which is 1018 pounds, displays a good margin of safety. But is it enough? Granted that the other strips tested higher than the 60 pound result we took to base our design upon, and therefore there may be additional reserve strength we are not counting, and the 30 pounds per square foot of snow load is "code" hence is probably conservative. Granted that we are assuming that all of the load is being carried in the tension arch direction, and that the compression arch direction carries no load. However, this roof will be used for a school class room, and we can not take a chance on its collapsing. We could use more layers than 4, or we close the school when the snow gets too deep. But then, also, the snow really will not pile up on the steep portions of the shell like we assumed, so we will likely not see 30 pounds per square foot of snow over the entire shell. However, the wind whipping up over the top of the shell may cause snow to drift more deeply on the down wind portions of the shell, exceeding 30 pounds per square foot in those regions. But again, as 30 pounds per square foot of snow is equivalent to about 40 to 50 inches of wet snow, (1-inch of water makes about 7-inches of wet snow) and the kids are only 40 to 50 inches tall, surely the school will be closed when the snow gets that deep.

These are all practical considerations. Let's decide to use only the 4 layers of fabric. See "Proof of the Design" on page 43 below.

The Slurry Coat

A slurry coat mix of cement and latex is painted onto the fiberglass fabric such that it penetrates throughout the layers of fabric and closes the void spaces. A common slurry coat mix is 1.5 to 2 parts cement to 1 part of liquid latex. The slurry is mixed to a lump-free, creamy consistency.

A slurry coat filler of fine screened sand can be added if desired, using a sand-to-cement ratio of up to 1.0, and with a maximum size sand particle of 0.4 times the fiberglass screen opening. If there are many screen layers, the sand size should be tested for blinding potential and decreased, or not used.

Rheomix 141 is a product which can be used to formulate the latex concrete material. It is manufactured by Degussa, and distributed by Master Builders, Inc. on a world-wide basis. The following descriptive information is taken largely from Rheomix 141 sales literature.[13]

Rheomix 141 is a styrene-butadiene co-polymer latex specifically designed for use with cement compositions. It is used in mortar and concretes as an admixture to enhance strength properties, increase resistance to water penetration, improve abrasion resistance and improve durability. It is used with cement as a reliable water-resistant bonding agent. Rheomix 141 is applicable to thin shell membrane construction.

The material has been developed specifically for use with Portland cements. As ordinary mortar dries out, voids are left which make it permeable and weaker. When Rheomix 141 is added to the mix, the Rheomix 141 particles bind together to form continuous films and strands, forming a co-matrix with the cement paste in the mortar. The latex material fills the voids, thus increasing the strength of the co-matrix, and its resistance to water penetration. Rheomix 141, combined with cement, produces an excellent adhesive, each component of the co-matrix complimenting the properties of the other.

Rheomix 141 is a milky white liquid, produced from styrene and butadiene by high pressure emulsion polymerization. It has a pH of 10.5, a specific gravity of 1.01, a mean particle size of 0.17 microns, and a butadiene-solids content of 40 percent by weight of the Rheomix 141 polymer. The latex consists of microscopic particles of synthetic rubber dispersed in an aqueous solution. Rheomix 141 modified mixes may be slightly darker than corresponding unmodified mixes.

A good slurry coat design mix using Rheomix 141 and fine sand is sand: cement, latex, and water in a 1.00 to 1.20 to 0.11 to 0.37 ratio by weight. The sand should be gap graded, with the largest sieve size 0.4 times the smallest screen opening.

Rhoplex MC-76, a comparable latex emulsion, is useful when an extended open time is desirable. This feature is especially beneficial in high-temperature, low-humidity environments such as are encountered in the southwestern United States, in Iraq, Iran and Afghanistan.

---

[13] Rheomix 141, http://www.mbt-saudi-arabia.com/datasheet/html/adformor/rmix141.html

Mixing

Mixing the latex slurry causes the latex to foam, and results in air entrap-ment. Air entrapment is to be avoided as it has an adverse effect on mate-rial properties. A defoaming agent can be used such as NOPCO NXZ, manu-factured by Diamond-Shamrock Corporation Process Chemicals Division, 350 Mt. Kemble Avenue, Morristown, NJ, 07960.

Mixing should preferably be carried out in an efficient, small sized concrete mixer if one is available. A pan type mixer such as a Creteangle is recom-mended. However, hand mixing in a wheel barrow or trough is the means most likely to be available at remote sites.

Make up the liquid latex taking into account the fact that the available liquids come in a variety of latex solids content, and the solids-to-cement ratio is of fundamental importance in producing quality concrete.

Work in small quantities. Charge the wheel barrow with the required quan-tity of sand and cement (say, two shovels full of cement, and two and a half shovels full of sand) and mix until the color of the dry mix is uniform. Then add latex liquid to wet the mix. To avoid excessive air entrapment, mix for a only a few minutes.

Finally, add the remaining latex solids and water mix slowly until the re-quired paste consistency, or coarse paste consistency is achieved. Owing to the strong plasticizing properties of latex formulations, rapid thinning can occur. Avoid adding excess liquid. This material sets up quickly, so achieve the right consistency and work rapidly, applying the slurry to the shell before the slurry turns to gel. The right consistency can be identified by the readi-ness of the slurry to ooze through the fabric and balloon up on the opposite side.

Do not use sea sand because of the salt content. Use dry river sand free of organic material.

Application Techniques

Using a stiff brush work the bonding slurry well into the fabric, ensuring that no pinholes are visible. Do not apply the bonding slurry at a thickness in ex-cess of 2 mm. (1/16") If a second coat is necessary, it must be applied after the first coat is touch dry. Brush the slurry coat onto the fabric until droplets of mix are extruded out of the back side of the fabric. Brush these droplets out to fill the fabric of the screen from both sides. Thoroughly brush the slurry coat into the fabric stapled to the edge and ridge members to ensure wetting and bonding to the underlying wood surfaces.

On vertical surfaces, several coats can be applied in fairly rapid succession, usually within 15 to 30 minutes of the previous coat. Brush to close the surface. Alternatively, allow the first coat to dry overnight then apply another coat.

Curing

Rheomix® 141 literature recommends that you moist cure the slurry coat application for 24 hours and then allow it to dry out slowly. The literature says this initial curing is necessary to provide good curing conditions for the hydration of the Portland cement. Then the latex mortar must be allowed to dry out and skin over to permit the latex particles to join together to form the continuous films and strands.

This writer has found that dry curing of latex products in latex concrete construction appears adequate, in contrast to the wet curing recommended for normal concrete. The latex skins over rapidly, trapping water within the matrix, allowing hydration of the cement to occur by the entrapment.

The Heavy Latex Concrete Coat

The latex concrete coat applied on top of the slurry coat is the flexural and compressive load bearing coat of the latex concrete membrane. The saddle shaped HP surface can be considered as a concave upward curve operating in tension, the tension being carried in the fiberglass fabric, and a concave downward curve operating in compression, the compression being carried in the latex concrete. The concave upward tension arch delivers tensile loads to the frame perimeter members. The concave downward curve is a compression arch delivering compressive loads to the frame members. The resulting tension and compression at the perimeter produces shear in the shell surface, and puts all of the frame members into axial compression.

The *latex solids to cement* ratio in latex mortars and concretes is important in developing proper strength and adhesive properties of the mix. The latex is the primary adhesive and sealer.   Mixes which specify latex <u>liquid</u> to cement ratio obscure the point that the latex *solids* content of the latex milk is a variable between manufacturers, and the latex *solids*-to-cement ratio is the primary determinant of the desired properties. Latex solids-to-cement ratios typically are in the range of 0.10 to 0.15.

Considering two different but usable specifications for latex concrete mixes, and that Portland cement (PC) comes in 94 pound bags (one cubic foot of cement per bag), and latex, for example Rohm and Haas MC-76 (Philadelphia, PA 19108) comes in 5 gallon buckets and 55 gallon barrels, the two mix specifications are:

- **Mix No. 1:** Cement, sand, MC-76, water: 1.0, 2.6, 0.14, 0.40 or 3 bags of cement, 733 pounds of sand, 10 gallons of MC-76, and 8 gallons of water.

- **Mix No. 2:** Cement, sand, MC-76, water: 1.0, 2.6, 0.11, 0.40 or 2 bags of cement, 489 pounds of sand, 5 gallons of MC-76, and 6 gallons of water.

With MC-76 being 47 percent solids and 53 percent water, the latex solids-to-cement and water-to-cement ratios can be calculated as follows:

Mix No. 1: Cement, sand, MC-76, water: 1.0, 2.6, 0.14, 0.40 or 3 bags of cement, 733 pounds of sand, 10 gallons of MC-76, and 8 gallons of water.

Weight of latex solids = 47 percent solids x 62.4 pounds per cubic foot x specific gravity of latex solids of 1.01, times 10 gallons, divided by 7.48 gallons per cubic foot gives

- **Weight Latex solids** = 0.47(62.4)1.01(10) / 7.48 = 39.6 pounds in 10 gallons.

- **Weight of cement** = 94 pounds per sack x 3 sacks = 282 pounds in 3 sacks.

- **Ratio of latex solids to cement by weight** = 39.6 / 282 = 0.14

- **Weight of water** = 0.53(62.4)10 / 7.48 + 8 x 62.4 / 7.48 = 44.2 + 66.7 = 110.9 lbs

- **The water/cement ratio by weight** = 110.9 / 282 = 0.39

Mix No. 2:   Cement, sand, MC-76, water: 1.0, 2.6, 0.11, 0.40 or 2 bags of cement, 489 pounds of sand, 5 gallons of MC-76, and 6 gallons of water gives

Weight of latex solids = 47 percent solids x 62.4 pounds per cubic foot x specific gravity of latex solids of 1.01, times 5 gallons, divided by 7.48 gallons per cubic foot, or

- Weight Latex solids = 0.47(62.4)1.01(5) / 7.48   =   19.8 pounds in 5 gallons.

- Weight of cement = 94 pounds per sack x 2 sacks = 188 pounds in 2 sacks.

- Ratio of latex solids to cement by weight = 19.8 / 188 = 0.105

- Weight of water = 0.53(62.4)5 / 7.48 + 6 x 62.4 / 7.48
                     = 22.1 + 50.1 = 72.2 lbs.

- The water/cement ratio by weight   = 72.2 / 188 = 0.38

Note: If the sand is not dry, any water in the sand must be deducted from the water volume cited.

You will find that unless you have a lot of help, the above mix designs produce batches of latex concrete too large to use. They are reduced to wheel barrel sized mix designs as follows.

Mix No. 1:   Cement, sand, MC-76, water: 1.0, 2.6, 0.14, 0.40 or 3 bags of cement, 733 pounds of sand, 10 gallons of MC-76, and 8 gallons of water,

Reduced Amounts: Use a quarter of a bag of cement, 60 pounds of dry sand (about a half a cubic foot), 3-1/3 quarts of MC-76, and 2-2/3 quarts of water. Mix the MC-76 and water separately. Mix more than the total of 6 quarts so that you can add it to the mix slowly to get the right consistency, but do not use it all.

Mix No. 2: Cement, sand, MC-76, water: 1.0, 2.6, 0.11, 0.40 or 2 bags of cement, 489 pounds of sand, 5 gallons of MC-76, and 6 gallons of water,

Reduced Amounts: Use half a bag of cement, one cubic foot of dry sand, 5 quarts of MC-76, and 6 quarts of water.

A Sample Latex Concrete Specification

The final latex concrete coat should have a latex polymer solids-to-cement ratio of between 0.10 and 0.15, a water-to-cement ratio of not more than 0.45, and a sand-to-cement ratio of about 2.5. The sand should be gap graded, if possible, with the largest fraction no larger than a No. 8 sieve, the medium fraction: No. 50 sieve, and the smallest fraction no smaller than a No. 100 sieve.

Rheomix® 141 Latex Concrete Properties

Table 1   Rheomix® 141 Physical Properties

+Typical Compressive Strength	40 N/mm² dependent on cement used and workability
+Typical Tensile Strength	Up to 6.5 N/mm² dependent on cement used and workability
+Typical Flexural Strength	Up to 13 N/mm² dependent on cement used and workability
Freeze thaw resistance	Excellent
Water vapor permeability	Less than 4 gm/m²/24hr, through 11 mm thick test piece*
Adhesion	Excellent to concrete, steel, brick, glass
Coefficient of Thermal Expansion	-20°C to +20°C: 12.8×10^{-6} +20°C to +60°C: 12.9×10^{-6}
Chemical Resistance	Resists mild acids, alkalis, sulphates, chlorides, urine, dung, lactic acid, sugar
Shrinkage during cure	0.01% to 0.02%
Resistance to water under pressure of 30m head	Excellent – no water through a 15 mm thick test piece.*

- indicates strengths are typical. Variation in cement used and workability can give increased strengths.
- Rheomix 141 added at 10 ltr / 50 kg cement.
- One Newton is 0.22481 pounds. One pound is approximately 4.5 Newtons.

The above properties of latex concrete are based on a 3:1 sand/cement mix in which 10 liters (2.7 gallons) of Rheomix 141 per 50 kg of Type 1 OPC cement have been incorporated. (10 liters and 50 kg are 2.7 gallons and 110 pounds, restively.)

Proof of the Design

In constructing a school building in a remote village, it is likely that you will build many shell roofs for the complex. It is recommended that at least one shell be built, and the roof test loaded to determine its collapse strength. The writers have found that long cloth bags, 4 to 6-inches in diameter and 5 to 8 feet long, filled with sand, can be loaded on a sloping roof surface, and will tend to stay put if stacked from the lower sides to the higher. Some bags may need to be tied high on the slope to stay in place. One steeply sloping shell was loaded with automobile inner tubes cut through and filled with sand. The bags were weighed as they are stacked onto the roof so that the total applied load was known.

First load the roof to the design load (say, the 30 pounds per square foot for snow load) and let the roof sit over night. Then load the roof to half again that amount, and let the roof sit over night. If possible, avoid being on the roof during the later stages of loading due to the possibility of collapse. If the structure is still standing, load the roof continuously until collapse occurs, and re-weigh the bags as they are removed to obtain a second check on the total weight the roof carried.

Problems and Solutions

- Always prewet a dry surface with latex slurry before applying latex modified concrete.
- Never apply Rheomix 141 modified concrete to a slurry coat that has dried.
- Always use fresh, cool, cement and sharp, clean, well graded aggregate, free of excessive fines.
- Keep mixing time to a minimum.

- Until the user becomes familiar with its workability, the appearance of Rheomix 141 modified mix is deceptive. When of the correct consistency it may appear to be too dry. However, it will be found that it can be compacted satisfactorily.
- Avoid using excessive water in a latex slurry or concrete mix...
- Do not over-brush, and avoid rebrushing.
- Protect from too rapid drying out.
- All tools should be cleaned with water immediately after use.
- If cleaning is delayed, use of soap and coarse wire wool may be helpful.
- Solvents such as white spirit can be used to remove partially hardened mortar.

Safety Precautions for Workers

- Avoid contact with eyes and prolonged contact with skin.
- During application always wear gloves, eye glasses and appropriate clothing to minimize contact.
- In case of contact with eyes, immediately flush with plenty of water for at least 15 minutes.
- Should skin contact occur, wash immediately with soap and water.
- Seek the advice of a physician should symptoms persist.
- When brushing the underside of a slurry coated shell, wear goggles, and a hard hat or shower cap to avoid getting the slurry in your eyes and hair.

Field Testing of Construction Techniques

The materials and formulations discussed above are varied, as a number of ways can be found to create these membrane structures. Thus the discussion has been general. It is recommended that throughout the design phase, the designers and the fabricators work together to try out different techniques and design mixes. Engineers seeking to introduce this construction methodology in remote sites are well advised to work out the production problems, and refine their techniques by building reduced scale working models of the final structure at home, prior to traveling to the remote site. While the construction work can largely be accomplished by unskilled labor, the direction of the construction project should be under the control of a creative person experienced in the materials and their application. Play around with the mix designs and construction techniques at home to avoid delays and failures in the field.

Students involved in Engineers Without Borders projects currently being encouraged in the United States are strongly advised (1) to first visit the site to make contacts, shake hands and to obtain permissions and commitments, then (2) to work with the contacts to identify materials and supplies, then (3) to design and build the project at least in model form at their home universities, then (4) return to the site for final construction and implementation.

It is imperative that the student be working with a knowledgeable, committed person at the site who agrees to carry through on work completion, and be available for on-site problem solving.

Chapter E

Stress Analysis

The purpose of this chapter is to present the engineering aspects of latex concrete shell roof design, and techniques for solving for the forces in the members.

General Configuration:

The sketches below show some of the configurations which can be assembled using LC HP shells.

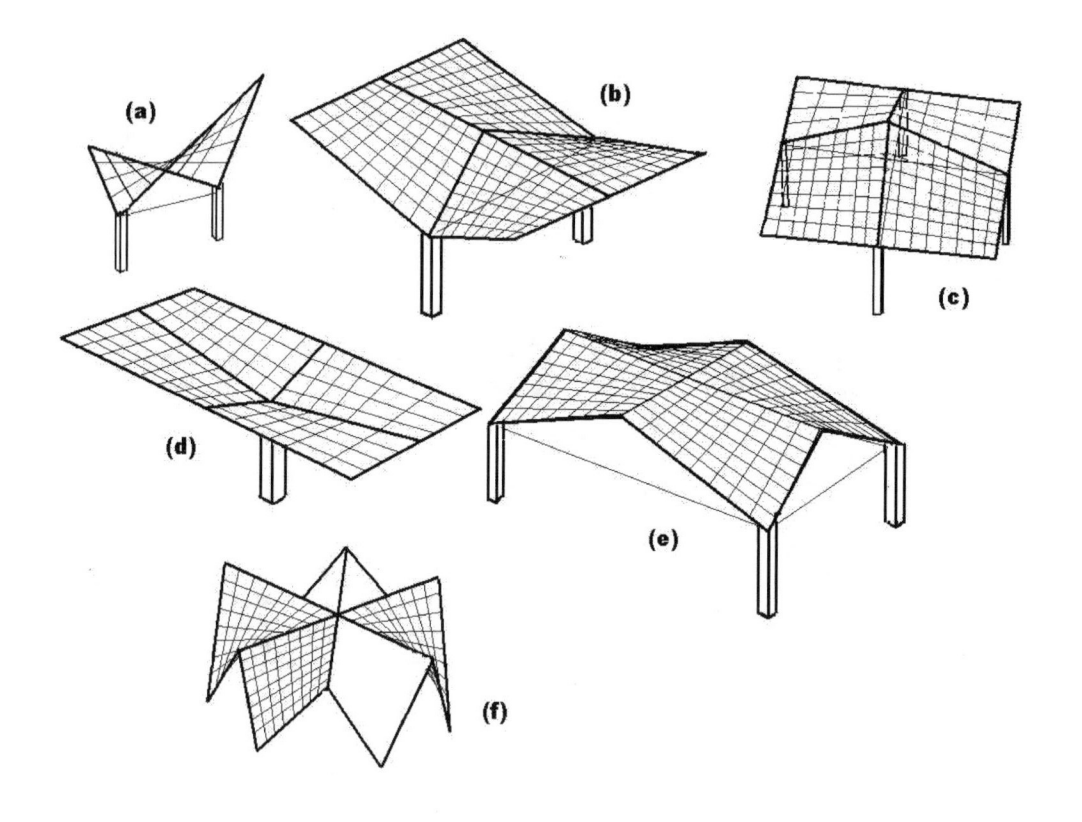

Figure 1 - Six Example Hypar Roof Structures

The simple shell shown as (a) in Figure 1 is a single shell with four edge members. By changing its proportions and lowering its peak, it could be the left-most shell in the four-shell roof shown as (c), or any of the surfaces shown in (f). The positions of the support columns have changed, (d) being supported on a single column in the center of the structure, and (f) being supported on six perimeter points. In each of the cases shown, the roof still carries its surface applied loads to edge members, and thence to the columns, then to the ground.

The surfaces carry their loads by membrane tension and compression in the directions of the diagonals, and in pure shear in the directions parallel to the edge members. The surfaces do not transmit their loads by bending, hence, they can be thin and light weight. This lack of bending is the reason why the roofs can have such wonderful long spans. The normal-concrete four HP shell roof shown in the photograph below is an example of this structural beauty.

Figure 2 - 180-Foot Span HP – Normal Reinforced Thin shell Concrete
The Broadmoor Pavilion, Colorado Springs, Colorado
Shell Designed by Milo S. Ketchum

this large shell is the topic of this chapter.

The four HP shells deliver their loads to the edge members which then deliver their loads to the corner columns, resulting in open, column-free interior spaces. The structural analysis of small, latex concrete roofs similar to this large shell is the topic of this chapter.

Shell Load Carrying Mechanism

Consider the shell surface ABOHA shown in Figure 3. The sides OH and OB are horizontal. The Z-axis is vertical. The line Ed, in traveling from OH to BA, generates a hyperbolic paraboloidal surface, by definition. The distance down from the HOB plane to the shell surface is given by the dimension, z. Knowing z for any point on the surface defines the surface and gives us a way to determine any dimension from the plane down to the surface.

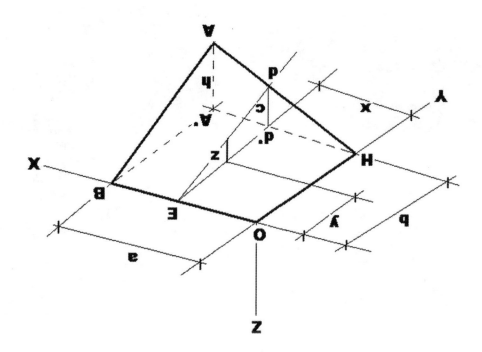

Figure 3 – Shell Surface Geometry

By similar triangles,

$$c/h = x/a \qquad \text{or} \qquad c = xh/a$$

Similarly in triangle Ed'd,

$$z/c = y/b$$

from which we get

$$z = yc/b = (y/b)(xh/a) = (h/ab) xy = kxy \qquad \text{Eq-1}$$

where $k = h/ab$, a constant.

The geometry of the parabolic curve of the shell surface extending from O to A can be shown graphically. If we calculate the distance z_c to the surface in the precise center of the shell where $x = a/2$ and $y = b/2$, then

$$z_c = k(a/2)(b/2) = k\, ab/4 = (h/ab)(ab/4) = h/4 \qquad \text{Eq-2}$$

This is true for all parabolas and is a useful property to know for HP geometry.

The arch from O to A is shown in Figure 4 below. The shell surface passes through points O and A, and at its middle passes through the point at $h/4$ below the horizontal plane. As the arch is a parabola, it is tangent to the horizontal plane at O (line Og), and is tangent to the line gA at A. This defines the shape and it can be scaled to get any other dimension desired. In shell action, this concave downward arch operates in pure compression.

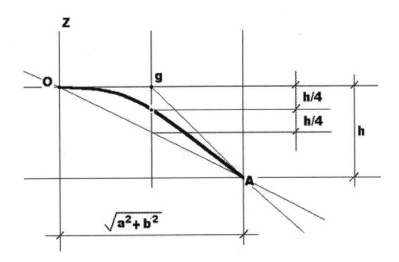

Figure 4 – The Geometry of the Shell Diagonal Midline OA.

Similarly, as shown in Figure 5, the geometry of the midline of the shell between H and B can be drawn. Note that the shell surface is tangent at H and B to the lines passing through point j. This concave upward shell midline arch operates in pure tension.

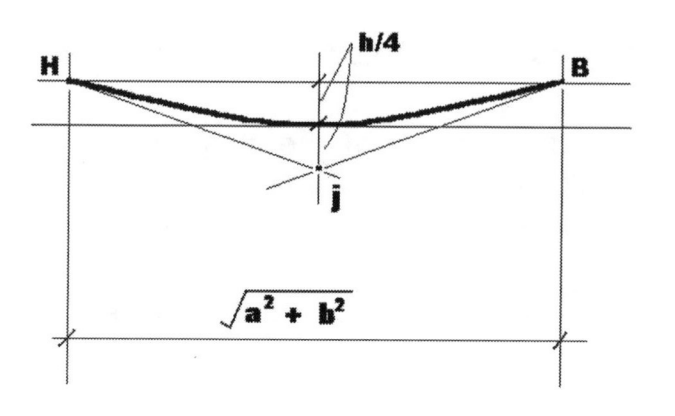

Figure 5 – The Geometry of the Shell Diagonal Midline HB.

Compression Forces in the Shell

As the stresses in the membrane at A, B, O and H lie in the surface, they are tangent to the shell surface at the edge members. Therefore the directions of the forces at the four corners lie along the tangents shown in the diagrams, Og and Ag in Figure 4, and along Hj, and Bj in Figure 5. Approximations of these forces can be obtained by considering a unit width of shell lying along the two diagonals:

The Compression Diagonal

Referring to Figure 6, if we assume that the weight of the unit width strip of the shell surface shown in Figure 4 is carried only in the compression arch, then summing the forces in the vertical direction in Figure 6 gives us:

$$C_A \sin phi = wS = W \hspace{3cm} \text{Eq-3}$$

> where sin phi is the slope of the line Ag, w is the unit weight of the surface of the shell (the latex concrete) in pounds per square foot, S is the length of the arch in feet, and C_A is the force in pounds per linear foot applied by the shell to the edge member at A.

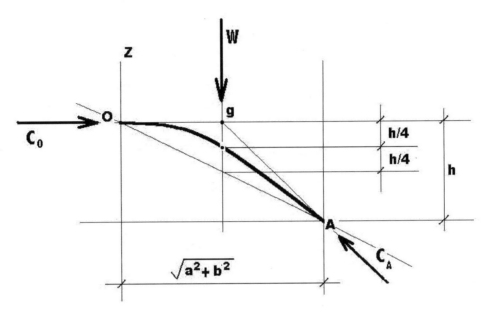

Figure 6   Forces on Shell Strip

Slope of gA is $\sin phi = h / ([0.5 \sqrt{(a^2 + b^2)}]^2 + h^2)^{1/2}$

$\sin phi = 2h / \sqrt{a^2 + b^2 + 4h^2}$ **and**

$C_A = wS (\sqrt{a^2 + b^2 + 4h^2}) / 2h$ **Eq-4**

S can be approximated as the average of the lengths OgA and OA.

$S = 0.5 (Og + gA + OA)$ **Eq-5**

where $Og = 0.5 \sqrt{(a^2 + b^2)}$

$gA = \sqrt{(0.5 \sqrt{(a^2 + b^2)})^2 + h^2} = 0.5 \sqrt{a^2 + b^2 + 4h^2}$

$OA = \sqrt{a^2 + b^2 + h^2}$

Considering the 10x10x4 LC HP shell, these dimensions become:

$Og = 0.5 \sqrt{(a^2 + b^2)} = 0.5 \sqrt{200)} = 7.071'$

$gA = 0.5 \sqrt{a^2 + b^2 + 4h^2} = 0.5 \sqrt{100 + 100 + 64} = 0.5\sqrt{264} = 8.124'$

$$OA = \sqrt{a^2 + b^2 + h^2} = \sqrt{216} = 14.697'$$

If we approximate the length of the diagonal curved arch, S, as the average of the upper line O&A and the sloping line OA, then the length of S is:

$$S = 0.5 (O\&A + OA) = 0.5 (7.071' + 8.124' + 14.697') = 14.95 \text{ feet.}$$

A rigorous solution gives, S = 14.93 feet.   See Appendix B.

Returning to Equation 4, and assuming that we weighed a 12 inch by 12 inch section of the proposed latex concrete surface to be 4.4 pounds (pounds per square foot), then:

$$C_A = wS \sqrt{a^2 + b^2 + 4h^2} / 2h = 4.4 (14.95) \sqrt{(100+100+64)} / 8 = 134 \text{ pounds.}$$

This is the maximum compression to be expected in a one-foot width of the shell, and will occur at the base of the arch at A.

Similarly the horizontal force at O can be found from C_A by summing the forces in the horizontal direction on the free body shown in Figure 6.

$$C_o = C_A \cos phi = (wS \sqrt{a^2 + b^2 + 4h^2} / 2h) \cos phi \quad \text{and}$$

$$\cos phi = 0.5 \sqrt{(a^2+b^2)} / \sqrt{(0.5 \sqrt{(a^2+b^2)})^2 + h^2}$$

$$= \sqrt{(a^2+b^2)} / \sqrt{a^2 + b^2 + 4h^2}$$

$$C_o = C_A \cos phi = (wS \sqrt{(a^2+b^2)} / 2h) \qquad \text{Eq-6}$$

For the 10x10x4 LC HP shell,

$$C_o = (wS \sqrt{(a^2+b^2)} / 2h) = 4.4 (14.95) (14.14) / 8 = 116 \text{ pounds}$$

per foot of width in compression at the crown.

Summarizing the Analysis for Compression Forces

The compression forces, in a unit width of the example shell taken along the compression diagonal, are 116 pounds per foot of width at the crown at point O, and 134 pounds per foot of width at point A at the base of the arch.

Note: The above analysis has assumed that all of the load is being carried by the compression arch, OA, that none of the load is carried by the tension arch, HB, and we have solved for the maximum values, C_A and C_O in a one-foot strip of the shell framing from O to A.

Giving no credit to the load carrying capacity of the shell in tension is conservative, possibly by a factor of 2 in a normally functioning shell. However, a shell which has been damaged by cutting the membrane partially away from the edge members may well act like a simple compression arch. Such cutting could occur by way of vandalism, fire or warfare.

The Tension Diagonal

Let us solve for the maximum tension in the shell along the tension diagonal H-B using a similar conservative approach. Assume all of the load is carried by the tension arch. A one foot wide strip of shell taken along the tension diagonal is illustrated in Figure 5 above, and as a force diagram in Figure 7 below.

By symmetry we know that T_H is equal to T_B.

By summing the forces in the vertical direction on the free body shown in Figure 7, we get:

$$2\,T_H \sin phi = wS, \quad \text{where } \sin phi = 2(h/4) / \sqrt{(0.5\sqrt{(a^2+b^2)})^2+(h/2)^2} \qquad \text{Eq-7}$$

$$\sin phi = h / \sqrt{a^2 + b^2 + h^2}$$

$$S = \tfrac{1}{2}(HB + HjB) = \tfrac{1}{2}(\sqrt{(a^2+b^2)} + \sqrt{a^2 + b^2 + h^2}) \qquad \text{Eq-8}$$

$$S = \tfrac{1}{2}(\sqrt{200} + \sqrt{216}) = 14.42 \text{ feet}$$

$$T_H = T_B = wS\sqrt{a^2 + b^2 + h^2} / 2h \qquad \text{Eq-9}$$

$$= 4.4\,(14.42)\,(14.70) / 8 = 116 \text{ pounds per foot of width.}$$

116 pounds per foot is the maximum tensile force in the tension diagonal.

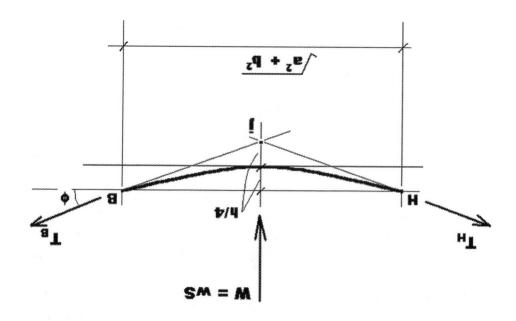

Figure 7   Forces Applied to the Tension Diagonal

The tension, T_m, in the surface at midspan of the arch HB is the horizontal component of T_H.

$$T_m = T_H \cos phi = T_H \ \{0.5\sqrt{(a^2+b^2)}\} / \sqrt{[(0.5\sqrt{(a^2+b^2)})^2 + (h/2)^2]}}$$

$$T_m = T_H \ \sqrt{a^2+b^2} / \sqrt{a^2+b^2+h^2} = wS \ \sqrt{(a^2+b^2)} / 2h \qquad \textbf{Eq-10}$$

$$T_m = 4.4 \ (14.42)\ (14.14) / 8 = 112 \quad \text{pounds per foot of width.}$$

Summary of the Tension Arch Analysis

The arch tension in the shell, assuming that the compression arch is ineffective in carrying load, is 116 pounds per foot of shell width at H and B, and 112 pounds per foot of width at midspan.   If we assume that the concrete surface has no tensile strength, these values become the needed design tensile strength of the fiberglass screen contained within the concrete, when multiplied by an appropriate factor of safety.   If the shell is thin such that

the regions of arch compression undergo out of plane buckling, this arch tension analysis for the shell properly defines the load carrying mechanism of the shell.

Summary of Arch Force Equations

The Compression Diagonal

$$S = \tfrac{1}{2} \left(\sqrt{(a^2 + b^2)} + \sqrt{a^2 + b^2 + h^2} \right) \qquad\qquad \text{Eq-8}$$

$$C_A = wS \sqrt{a^2 + b^2 + 4h^2} \,/\, 2h \qquad\qquad \text{Eq-4}$$

$$C_0 = wS \sqrt{(a^2 + b^2)} \,/\, 2h) \qquad\qquad \text{Eq-6}$$

$$\text{where} \quad S = \tfrac{1}{2} (Og + gA + OA) \qquad\qquad \text{Eq-5}$$

$$Og = \tfrac{1}{2} \sqrt{(a^2 + b^2)}$$

$$gA = \tfrac{1}{2} \sqrt{a^2 + b^2 + 4h^2}$$

$$OA = \sqrt{a^2 + b^2 + h^2}$$

The Tension Diagonal

$$T_H = T_B = wS \sqrt{a^2 + b^2 + h^2} \,/\, 2h \qquad\qquad \text{Eq-9}$$

$$\text{where} \quad S = \tfrac{1}{2} \left(\sqrt{(a^2 + b^2)} + \sqrt{(a^2 + b^2 + h^2)} \right) \qquad\qquad \text{Eq-8}$$

$$T_M = T_H \cos phi = wS \sqrt{(a^2 + b^2)} \,/\, 2h \qquad\qquad \text{Eq-10}$$

where the arch forces are defined in Figures 6 and 7.

Note: We have deliberately been conservative by calculating values for shell reactions assuming that all of the weight is carried by either the compression arch, or the tension arch, *but not both*. The shell forces and hence edge member loads will be approximated in true shell action if we assume both carry half of the load, hence the above values are conservative by a factor of two.

The Assumption of Parabolic Shape in the Above Discussion

In this presentation we have somewhat blindly accepted that the surface with which we are working is a hyperbolic paraboloid formed by a rotating and translating straight line. This is nearly precisely correct. However, the geometric shape of a hyperbolic paraboloid is slightly different than the shape of a surface formed by the gravitational weight of a weighted fully flexible membrane. Consider the two sketches shown in Figure 8.

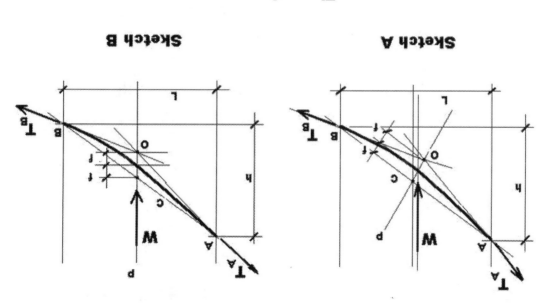

Sketch A   Sketch B

Figure 8

We formed the hyperbolic paraboloid by taking a line in space and translating it along a midline, while rotating it in space about that line. See Figure 1, page 12, of this manual. This would be the surface described by an airplane propeller rotating about its axis at a constant rotational speed, while translating along the straight line of flight of the airplane. Line CD in Figure 1 shown on page 12 would be the axis of flight of the airplane, and lines AB and EF would be successive positions of the propeller at two differing instances of time.

However, if we take the direction of flight of the airplane to be the line AE from page 12, and the length AB to be half of the radius of the propeller, then line AB is still describing a hyperbolic surface ABFEA, but the line BF is being generated along a helix, and is not a straight line. Both surfaces are hyperbolic, but with respect to differing reference axes.

As shown in Sketch A of Figure 8 above, the shape is a function solely of geometry, while in Sketch B, the parabolic shape is a function of the direction of gravity, and is not arbitrary. In Sketch A the shell is symmetrical about the midline OP and the weight W passes through the centroid of that midline. In Sketch B, we are assuming that the shape of the midline is approximated by a link chain hanging under gravity, and the line of action OP is vertical due to gravity. The total weight of the chain, W, is a vertical force acting through the midpoint of the span, L. (Don't get me started on catenaries.) In both cases, the shell is forming a parabola, and it is upon that assumption that we are basing our mathematical analysis for surface tension.

Shell Load-Carrying Mechanism and Delivery of Force to Edge Members

In the above discussion we have conservatively assumed first that the compression diagonal arch carried all of the load in a 1-foot wide strip, then that the tension diagonal arch carried all of the load in a 1-foot wide strip. This led to conservative estimations of the forces in the shell, and can be used for design of shells where safe long term field performance is potentially in jeopardy. The structural adequacy of any shell can and should be verified by proof loading to a gravity load equal to twice the maximum expected load the shell will see in service, and to laterally applied loads of 1.5 times the maximum wind or earthquake load to be expected.

Let us turn our attention to the normal performance of the shell wherein it carries its loads by membrane tension and compression acting simultaneously.

Referring to Figure 9 on the next page, the distance, z, from the horizontal plane down to the surface of the HP shell is given by:

$$z = kxy \qquad \text{where} \quad k = h/ab$$

Figure 10, also shown on the following page, is an element taken out of the shell surface at point z in Figure 9. The element is in static equilibrium under the influences of the forces, including a gravity load, w(dx)(dy), that are applied to it. The lateral faces of the element are oriented parallel to the sides a and b of the full shell OABC.

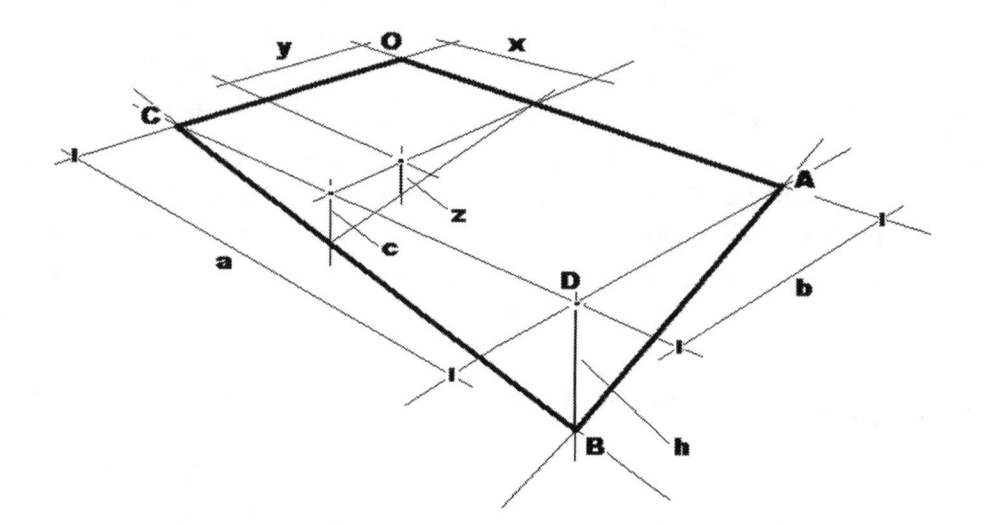

Figure 9   The Shell Surface OABC

The direct stresses, s_x and s_y, and the shear stresses, v_{xy} and v_{yx}, when multiplied by the areas of the lateral sides of the element are forces which hold the element in equilibrium, resist the transmitted arch loads, and the weight of the element.

It is to be noted that if we sum the moments about the vertical axis through the center of the element shown in Figure 10, the stresses, s and v, create canceling moments about this axis. Therefore, the shear stresses, v_{xy} and v_{yx} on the adjacent element faces are equal to each other.

$$V_{xy} \ = \ V_{yx}$$

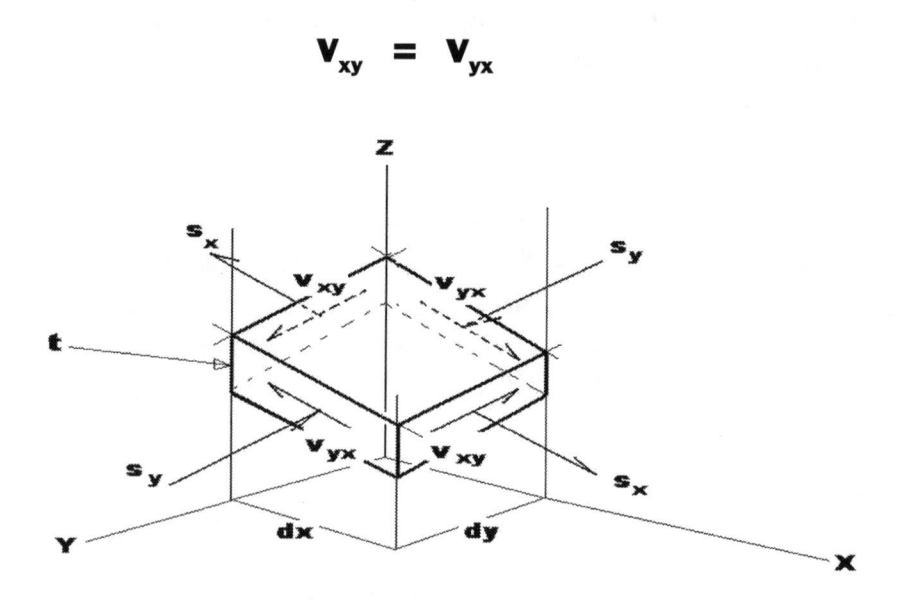

Figure 10   A Square Element Taken Out of the Surface at Z

Similarly, if we extend the element up the slope until it is at an edge, the edge has no externally applied direct stress in it. Therefore the direct stress values, s_x and s_y, are both zero on all elements whose lateral faces are oriented parallel to the lateral edges on the shell. See sketch (a) in Figure 11.

If we rotate the element shown in Figure 11 (a) 45 degrees about the z-axis we get the element shown in plan as (b) in Figure 11. The forces parallel to the two shell diagonals are resolved into shear forces on an element oriented at 45 degrees to the diagonals. Thus, large direct stresses occur in the shell in the diagonal directions, and only shear stresses occur in the shell in elements taken parallel to the edge members.

Considering the element in 11(c) below, and summing the forces in the horizontal direction, the shear forces on the left are counteracted by the force due to direct stress on the right.

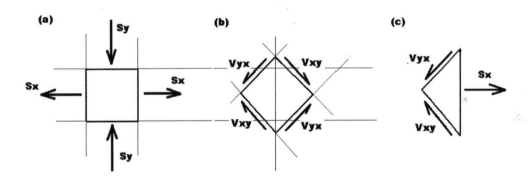

(a)   (b)   (c)

Stress in the Diagonals   Stress Parallel to the Edges

Figure 11   Rotated Shell Elements and Static Equilibrium

$$\text{Sum } (F_H) = 2 v_{xy} [(dx) t] \cos 45° - s_x [(1.414 \, dx) t] = 0$$

where t (dx) is the lateral area of the element over which the shear stress is applied, and t dx / cos 45° is the area over which the direct stress, S_x, is applied.

Therefore, $2 (v_{xy}) 0.707 - (s_x)1.414 = 0$, and

$$v_{xy} = s_x$$

Therefore, the direct and shear stress magnitudes in pounds per square inch (or forces in pounds per linear foot of shell) are equal.

As seen in the earlier analysis for arch action, the bending moment in the arch is zero, hence the thrust of the arch must at all times cancel the bend-ing considering the arch to be a beam spanning between the arch supports.

Considering the arch OA, (See Figure 12 below), and considering the force C_0, the center point of the span through which the total load W acts, and solving for the bending moment at that point, we get:

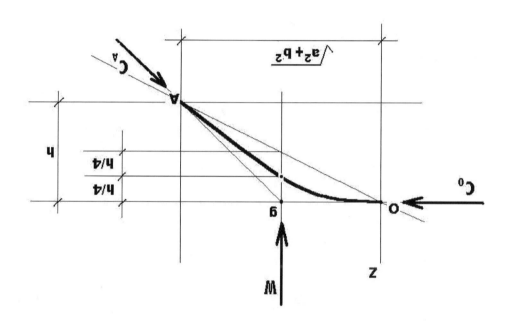

Figure 12 (same as Figure 6)

$$\text{Sum (M)} = C_0\,(h/4) - (wS/2)\,(\tfrac{1}{4}\sqrt{a^2 + b^2}) = 0$$

Therefore $\quad C_0 = wS\,\sqrt{a^2 + b^2}\,/\,2h,$

as we obtained before in Equation 6 on page 55.

Summing the moments around point A and setting it equal to zero gives the same equation. This property is useful in calculating arch reactions for a variety of shell configurations.

Edge Member Forces

Consider the forces delivered to the edge members by the arches. As shown in Figure 13, the forces applied by the arches in both tension and compression produce a pure shear force delivered to the edge member.

The magnitudes of the maximum values of the forces are given by the derived equations 4 through 10. These arch forces produce edge member shear causing the edge members to go into axial compression.

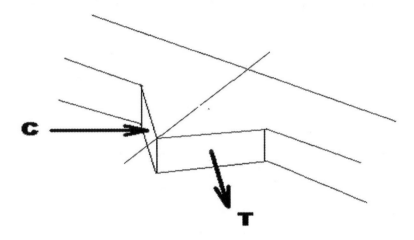

Figure 13   Arch Forces Applied at the Edge Members

The arch force magnitudes are a function of the span of each arch, and the span lengths vary from zero to a maximum in opposing directions. See Figure 14. Hence the compressive thrust of arches parallel to arch OA varies from a maximum at O and A to zero at H and B as the spans vary from a maximum to zero in length.

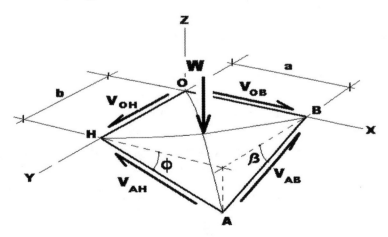

Figure 14   Shell Element Equilibrium

Similarly, the arch tension forces applied to the edge members is a maximum at H and B, and vary to zero at O and A. Thus, the resultant axial forces in the edge and ridge members are considered to build up uniformly along the length of each member.

The surface area of a relatively flat shell can be taken as the plan area of the shell.

Thus, Area = ab

The surface area of a steep shell is developed in Appendix C, hence the weight, W, in the above analysis will be larger due to the larger actual surface area.

Calculation of Edge Member Forces

The sum of the moments of these edge shears about the z-axis through O is zero. Please refer to Figure 14. Therefore:

$$V_{AH} \, b \cos phi = V_{AB} \, a \cos beta,$$

$$V_{AH} \, b \, a / \sqrt{(a^2+h^2)} = V_{AB} \, a \, b / \sqrt{(b^2+h^2)}$$

$$V_{AH} = V_{AB} \, \sqrt{(a^2+h^2)} / \sqrt{(b^2+h^2)} \qquad\qquad \text{Eq-12}$$

Summing the forces on the shell in the vertical direction, we get:

$$\text{Sum } (F_v) = V_{AH} \sin phi + V_{AB} \sin beta - W = 0$$

$$\text{where} \quad \sin phi = h / \sqrt{a^2+h^2})$$

$$\sin beta = h / \sqrt{b^2+h^2})$$

and   W = the total weight of the shell plus its live load.

$$V_{AB} \, [\, (\sqrt{(a^2+h^2)} / \sqrt{(b^2+h^2)}) \,] \, [\, (h / \sqrt{(a^2+h^2)}) \,] + V_{AB} \, (h / \sqrt{(b^2+h^2)}) \,) = W$$

$$V_{AB} \, [\, h / \sqrt{(b^2+h^2)} + h / \sqrt{(b^2+h^2)} \,] = W$$

$$V_{AB} = W \sqrt{(b^2+h^2)} / 2h \qquad\qquad \text{Eq-13}$$

For our 10x10x4 HP LC shell, and using the approximation, Area = ab for relatively flat shells, we get:

$$\text{Weight, } W = (4.4 \text{ psf}) [(10+10)/2]^2 + 10 \times 10 \times 30$$
$$= 440 + 3000 = 3440 \text{ pounds.}$$

$$V_{AB} = [3440 \sqrt{116}) / 8] = 4630 \text{ pounds.}$$

$$V_{AH} = V_{AB} \sqrt{(a^2+h^2)} / \sqrt{(b^2+h^2)} = 4630 \text{ pounds, as } a = b. \qquad \text{Eq-14}$$

The equations for V_{CO} and V_{OA} can be obtained by summing the forces in their respective directions as shown in Figure 14.

$$\text{Sum } (F_y) = V_{OB} - V_{AH} \cos \text{phi} = 0$$

$$V_{OB} = V_{AH} [a / \sqrt{(a^2+h^2)}] = 4630 [10 / \sqrt{116}] = 4300 \text{ pounds.} \quad \text{Eq-15}$$

$$\text{Sum } (F_y) = V_{OH} - V_{AB} \cos \text{beta} = 0$$

$$V_{OH} = V_{AB} [b / \sqrt{(b^2+h^2)}] = 4630 [10 / \sqrt{116}] = 4300 \text{ pounds.} \quad \text{Eq-16}$$

Summary of Equations for Edge Members

Area = ab for relatively flat shells. For relatively steep shells, the shell area is:

$$\text{Area} = [(b+\sqrt{(b^2+h^2)} /4] [\sqrt{(b^2+h^2)} +(a^2/h) (\ln (bh+b\sqrt{(a^2+h^2)} - \ln (ab))] \qquad \text{Eq-12}$$

$$V_{AB} = W \sqrt{(b^2+h^2)} / (2h) \qquad\qquad \text{Eq-13}$$

$$V_{AH} = V_{AB} \sqrt{(a^2+h^2)} / \sqrt{(b^2+h^2)} = W \sqrt{(a^2+h^2)} / (2h) \qquad \text{Eq-14}$$

$$V_{OH} = V_{AB} [b / \sqrt{(b^2+h^2)}] \qquad = W \, b/2h \qquad\qquad \text{Eq-15}$$

$$V_{OB} = V_{AH} [a / \sqrt{(a^2+h^2)}] \qquad = W \, a/2h \qquad\qquad \text{Eq-16}$$

where the shear forces are defined in Figure 14.

Chapter F

Placing New Roofs On Existing Walls

The concept of placing latex concrete shell roofs on already existing walls was introduced earlier. The photograph which follows was used to assist in visualization of the concept.

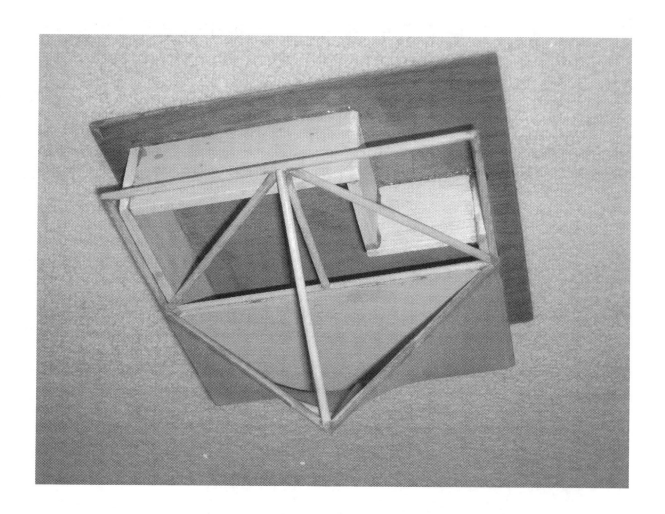

A Four Segment LC HP Roof Supported on Random Preexisting Walls

The writers would like to extend the concept to discuss methods of erection of such roofs.

Erection by Hand Labor

Walls without roofs are common in war torn villages, and in villages recently struck by high winds or hurricanes. The latex concrete HP shell is a useful, low cost roof construction for replacement of these roofs. Roofs can be built by hand in central areas of a town adjacent to the walls, then lifted into place by hand or light construction equipment, and anchored down.

The walls can be prepared by anchoring timber plates to the tops of the walls to receive the new roof construction. The timber plates can be anchored into the walls with anchors sufficient to resist wind uplift, or the roof assembly can be placed, and the roof anchored by running dead man tie downs into the soil, or by attaching the roofs onto new columns set in concrete. Consider the following method of erection.

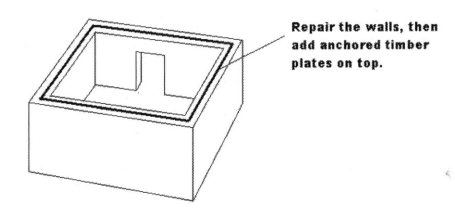

Repair the walls, then add anchored timber plates on top.

Figure 1 – Existing Walls

The roof can be built on the ground, and positioned adjacent to the walls, as shown in Figure 2 below. The roof is blocked off from the walls with a pivot frame of struts a-b-c-d. By pulling on the rope with a vehicle, the near edge of the roof can be lifted up until the edge b-d is lifted to the top of the wall line. When the weight of the roof edge is supported on the wall, the frame a-b-c-d can be removed. Depending on the materials of the wall, the bearing points of the ropes may need to be shimmed to prevent the ropes from sawing down through the wall during the pull. Additional hand lifting can be utilized.

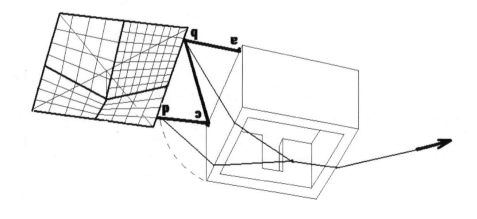

**Figure 2 – Roof positioned near walls, and blocked off
from the walls with a frame**

As shown in Figure 3 below, as the roof is being lifted additional struts e-f and g-h can be dropped into slit trenches, and affixed to the roof edge members. With additional pulling on the rope, the roof will be lifted on these new struts so that it can be slid onto the walls tops, as shown in Figure 4.

Hand labor will be needed to keep the roof from swinging to the side as it is being lifted from the position in Figure 3 to the position shown in Figure 4. Guy ropes affixed to the two lower corners of the roof will be needed during this phase.

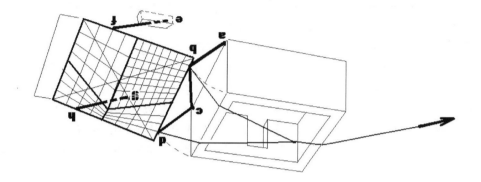

Figure 3 – Additional props are added to assist in lifting.

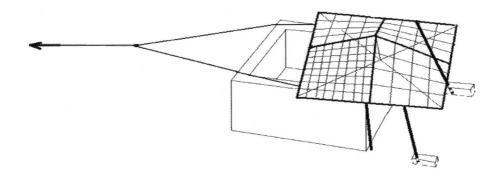

Figure 4 – Once lifted the roof can be slid into place and anchored.

It is practical as a modification to the above, to lift the roof until its edge rests on the top of the wall, then the frame a-b-c-d can be removed, and used as e-f-g-h.

Considerations

1. As can be noted in the initial photograph above, the plan area of the roof need not be the same as the plan area of the walls below. In the model, diagonal and cross members were added to the shell frame in the plane of its ceiling. These formed a structural grid allowing the shell weight to be carried to the walls, independent of where the walls may be. These diagonal and cross members can be made so heavy as to carry the full weight of the finished shell and its eventual superimposed live load (such as snow), or can be made so light as to only carry the weight of the shell when it has only its first coat of parging on it. Final loading can be carried by columns added under the joints and corners of the shell to transfer the gravity loads to the ground. Note that if columns are added, the walls are not being used structurally even though they may have considerable load carrying capacity.

2. Attachment of columns to edge members was discussed and sketched earlier. A sketch of the attachment for shell frames built with dimensional lumber is repeated below.

3. Pole columns can be attached using steel straps installed before parging, and nailed to the pole column after erection. See sketch on pole column attachment on next page.

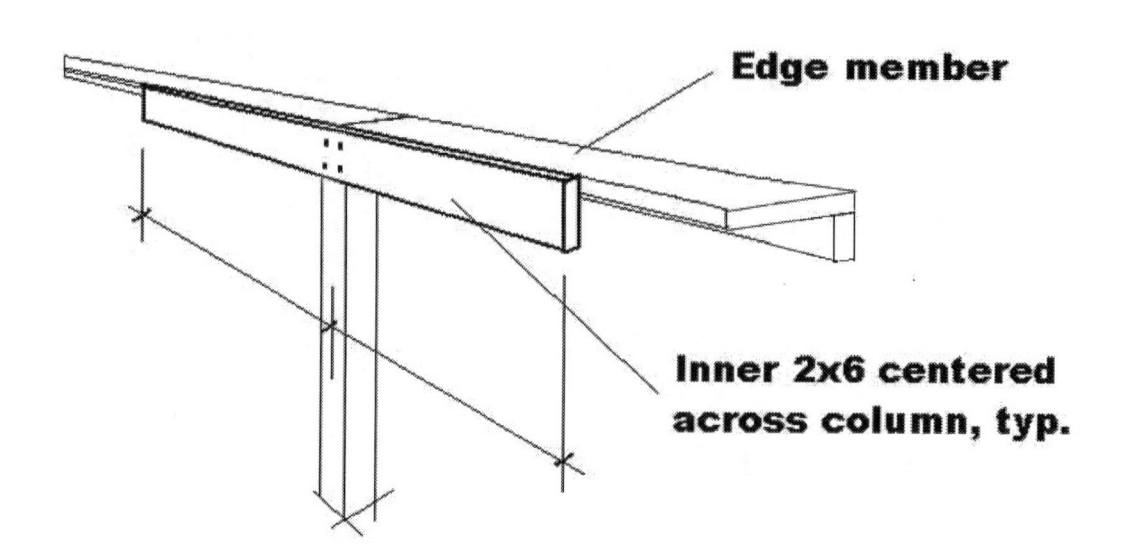

Figure 5 Slice Plate over Joint over Column

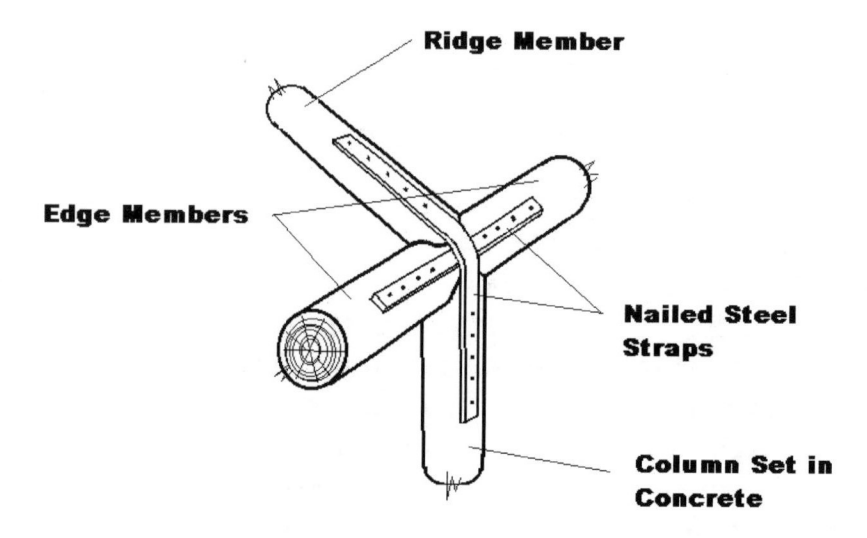

Figure 6   Joining Pole Shell at Column

4. Anchoring the shell down against wind up lift can be accomplished by running a cable or tendon from the shell edge member to a tie down buried in the ground. The tie down anchorage may be concrete poured into a hole in the ground.

5. The tie down weight may be estimated by assuming a horizontal wind load of 45 pounds per square foot of vertical projection of the roof

(hurricane loading at a 150 mph). For a shell 20 feet on each side, by 6 feet in rise, the vertical projection is 0.5 x 20 x 6 = 60 square feet. 45 pounds per square foot times 60 square feet is a lateral load of 2700 pounds applied at about half way up, or h/2 above the level of the top of the walls. In addition to this load, if the building is relatively open on the up-wind side, and fairly closed on the downwind side, such that the wind can enter and be trapped within, the uplift on the roof could approach 45 pounds per square foot on half of the interior roof area. If we approximate the structural action of the roof as it lifts off of the walls as a rotation of the roof about the top of the wall on the leeward side of the roof, resisted by a vertically downward anchorage load in the tendons on the windward side, the load in the middle tendon of three tendons would be:

$$T = \frac{1}{2} (2700 \times 3' / 20') + \frac{1}{2} (45 \times 20 \times 10) \, 5' / 20'$$

$$= 200 + 1250 = 1450 \text{ pounds per tendon.}$$

It can be seen that the majority of the high wind loading is caused by the wind being able to enter the building and blow it up and out. There are two scenarios available to reduce the wind loading on the roof during high winds. Either button the house up completely so that the wind can not enter, or open the house up completely on the down wind side so that the wind can get out as easily as is gets in. The latter may be the most practical in native construction.

If we design a single anchor for half of the above expected load, and anticipate that some damage to the roofs is unavoidable, the concrete anchor would have to weigh 760 pounds. At a unit weight of concrete of 140 pcf, this requires an anchor of say five cubic feet of concrete for each tendon. This can be obtained using an anchorage hole filled with concrete where the hole is 3-foot deep and 1½ feet in diameter. In freeze-thaw climates, the hole should be 4 feet deep, and filled to within 1-foot of the top with concrete, then backfilled with soil. The tie down anchorage cable should be waterproofed at and below grade.

Place such an anchor at each corner and at the center of each side of the shell. If the tie down is a vertical 6-inch diameter timber column in a 18-inch diameter hole filled with concrete, set the columns four feet into the ground.

As in all native construction, design for truly high winds is impractical. Our approach is to design it to resist significant wind loading, then tie it down so that it can be retrieved later.

6. Other techniques for getting the shell on top of the existing walls are:

a. Lift the shell with a crane, or helicopter, if available,

b. Lift the shell one corner at a time with a front end loader and props,

c. Lift the shell by hand labor when only the first latex slurry coat has been applied. A 20' x 20' shell at this stage of construction will weight only about 1000 pounds. The side of the shell nearest the wall can be lifted with say 6 to 10 men, and the roof leaned against the wall until its upper edge member clears the top of the wall. The shell can then be lifted and walked over the edge of the wall until the roof tilts over into a horizontal position balanced on top of the wall. When the shell is balanced on the walls, the shell can be shifted laterally into place incrementally by placing vertical struts under the lateral edges of the shell as done with the e-f-g-h struts discussed above, and shifting the roof by tipping the e-f-g-h struts over center.

d. Raise a heavy shell horizontally by lifting the shell fore and aft with a car jack under a center joint in the edge member, and shimming the adjacent edge members with pallets or other stable stack of materials as the edge members rise. Tether the shell laterally to avoid tip over of the pallets during the lift.

e. It is to be noted that ropes and lifting devices can be attached to the shell by simply puncturing the shell to receive the rope, then later patching the hole with fiberglass fabric and latex concrete.

Chapter G

Construction Ideas for Latex Concrete Habitat

HP Shells

Definition: Latex Concrete Habitat is low cost, permanent, virtually maintenance free housing for displaced people groups, built using local labor. It is made from:
- locally available wood framing materials,
- either locally available strong fabric or fiberglass fabric,
- liquid latex (available in any country which has a paint industry),
- Portland cement, and
- sand.

When a mixture of liquid latex, Portland cement and sand is hand troweled onto and through a stretched fabric and allowed to harden, a stiff, shell-like surface develops which is capable of carrying considerable load. It is low cost, waterproof, virtually maintenance free, and can be produced by local labor under the guidance of a single knowledgeable worker. It can be used for roofs and walls for housing. As housing, it is safe against wind, rain and earthquake, and can be portable for moving to alternate sites for erection. Latex concrete, as a "roofs-first" construction, can provide rapid replacement housing for a displaced community, and the self-help aspect of the construction can provide a community work project capable of uniting displaced people.

Assembly: In coating the surface of a stretched fabric, the first coat is a slurry of liquid latex, and Portland cement. This slurry coat is incorporated into the fabric, and care is taken to ensure that the fabric is completely wetted through. Thus the fabric needs to have a weave open enough to allow the slurry to be pushed through to the back side, and tight enough to allow the slurry to bridge and close the gap between the strands. If the slurry pours through the fabric too readily, add fine sand to the mix.

The back side is brushed smooth to guarantee a seal, to fill the fabric to develop bond, and to produce a water proof product. This attention to first coat application also allows the multiple layers of fabric to be bonded to each other to avoid gaps and openings.

Subsequent coats on the fabric are modified by adding sand to the latex-cement slurry. When sand is added to the slurry, the product is called *latex concrete.* Latex concrete is normally used for subsequent coats on shell roofs to strengthen them after they have been lifted and fitted into place as roof elements.

Other Uses: Other uses for the latex concrete construction are available. The latex-slurry-wetted fabric can be laid over existing native habitat such as hogans and yurts to add significant strengthening and durability. The hardened fabric can then also receive one or more layers of latex concrete.

The wetted fabric can be used to make grain storage bags, water storage tanks and dry toilet sanitation facilities. The latex slurry can be worked into the soil of a floor of a hut to harden it, and improve the health of the occupants through resistance to soil borne insects. The slurry or a latex sludge can be used to build roads by mixing the sludge with the soil, and roller compacting it in place.

Because of the waterproof nature of the latex-concrete construction, the material is ideal for making water tanks, water collection basins, pipes and conduits.

HP Configurations

General Definition: An HP shell is a surface generated by stretching fabric across a frame made by joining four edge members at their ends to form a rectangle, and warping the frame by lifting one or more corners as shown in Figure 1 below. It is also described as a surface generated by a line AB traveling along an axis CD perpendicular to the line, and rotating about the axis as it travels. The line AB moves along the axis CD until it reaches position EF. The surface so generated is called a *hyperbolic paraboloid*, or HP shell surface. If the frame ABFEA is formed using straight members such as timber poles, and a one-foot-wide strip of fabric is stretched from A to B and a second strip of fabric is stretched from A to E, overlapping the fabric at A, and the process is repeated with successive overlapping strips until the entire surface is covered, this HP fabric surface can be coated with a latex-cement (LC) slurry which will harden into an HP shell. This light weight LC-HP shell element can be used as a roof.

Single Shells: The shell ABFEA is a single shell. It can be supported on columns at A, B and E, or directly on the ground at points B and E, with a columnar prop at A. It can then be occupied as a home. Thus a light weight shell roof has been produced from four poles, a fabric, and a thin coating of latex-cement slurry.

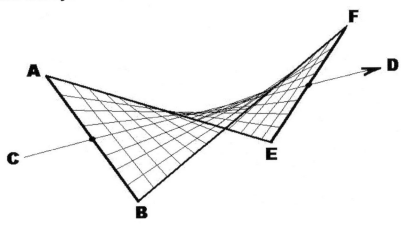

Figure 1 - Hyperbolic Paraboloid Surface

Multiple Shells: Four such LCHP shells can be joined together and set on columns to make the 4-shell roof structure shown in Figure 2 below. Thus a considerable area can be covered and used as habitat. It has been found that if such roofs are built for a displaced population, the people will move in under the roofs, and build their own walls. This is called *Roofs First* construction. The 4-shell roof is stable on its four columns, hence the walls can be placed anywhere in accordance with the wishes of the occupants.

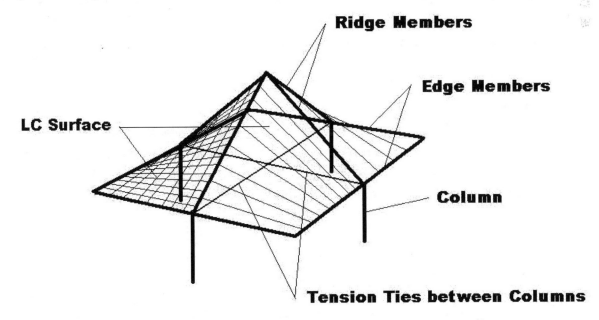

Figure 2 Four Shells on One Frame

Figure 3   Elementary School at Wardak Afghanistan

Wardak School: In the photograph shown above, three 4-element LCHP shells are shown in place on a school building in Wardak Afghanistan. These shells were built by Dr. George Nez as a demonstration for the local school district and sponsoring citizens. The roofs were built on preexisting mud walls. See Appendix A.

HP Construction

The details of shell roof construction are covered in chapters C and D. This "Ideas" chapter will be limited to selected ideas which can be incorporated into shell roof construction to demonstrate the freedom of choice available through thin shell latex concrete construction.

Methods of Joining Shells:

There are several ways to build a 4-shell roof. The four shells can be built separately as single shells as shown in Figure 1 above, and joined at the ridge beams by either of methods 1 or 2 sketched below, or they can be built together on a single, four quadrant frame as shown for Method 3 and discussed in Chapter C.

Method 1: Using nailer boards as a sandwich to improve the alignment of adjacent ridge members.

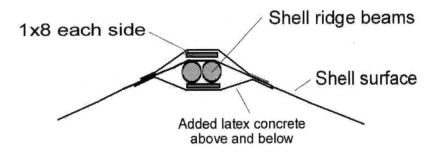

Figure 4 Framing for Misaligned Ridge Members

Align the shell ridge members, clad them with boards to force closer alignment, and nail the cladding boards in place. Cover the assembly with latex concrete.

Method 2: Tying the adjacent ridge members together directly.

Punch holes in the roof membrane and thread rope or latex slurry saturated fabric through the holes, tie the ends together below the shells, insert a short stick, and pull the shells tightly together by twisting the stick. When tight, nail the stick to one of the ridge members and enclose the space by adding parging to it under the shell surfaces.   Similarly lay a latex concrete membrane strip over the top of the edge members to seal the two shells together with a watertight seal.

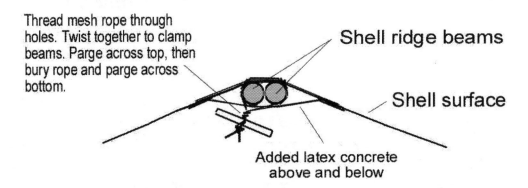

Figure 5 Framing for Aligned Ridge Edge Members

Method 3: A third technique which was used in the school roofs at Wardak is to build a 4-shell frame as one unit using common ridge members as shown in cross section below. This is best accomplished using dimensional lumber as discussed in chapter C.

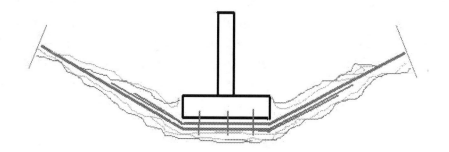

Figure 6 Combined Edge Member Construction

After the fabric is stapled in place over the common ridge members, the four surfaces are coated with first latex slurry, then latex concrete to produce the finished "four-element-one-frame" shell.

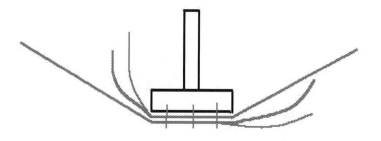

Figure 7 Finishing Combined Edge Member Construction

Configurations

Shown in Figure 8 below are six configurations of hyperbolic paraboloidal shells. Considering that HP shells can incorporate any number of shell elements, or combinations of shell elements, the variety from which to select is unlimited. The Wardak roofs were type (c) as shown below. Note that in Wardak they were supported on preexisting earthen walls instead of columns.

These shell combinations can be placed on columns, can bear directly on footings on the ground, or can be supported using a combination of columns and footings. Due to their light weight character, light weight as compared to most indigenous construction, attention must be paid to tying the shells down to prevent wind uplift and over turning.

The light weight characteristic however allows for almost any combination of supports which can be separate from the walls, hence the shells can be used to re-roof bombed out construction in war torn regions.

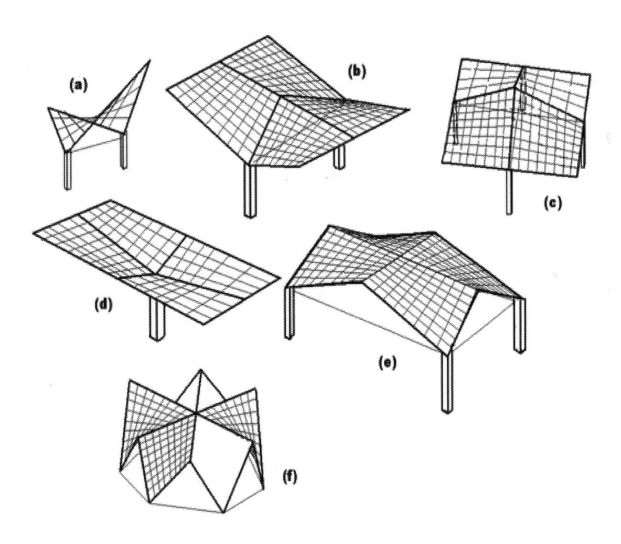

Figure 8 – Examples of HP Shell Roofs

Application of Slurry

In Chapters C and D, the builder was told to stretch the fabric over the edge and ridge members of the roof frame, and staple it down. Then he was to mix latex liquid and Portland cement to get a slurry, then to apply the slurry to the fabric using brushes. After brushing the slurry onto the shell surface, the builder was asked to add sand to the slurry to make a latex concrete, and to spread the wet concrete on the hardened shell surface using a broom.

This all requires access to the roof surface of a potentially fairly large shell structure. So the first idea presented in this chapter is leaving a work hole high in the shell as shown in Figure 9 below. The work hole has been found useful by construction workers who work standing on scaffolding or on a ladder. Pouring the fluid concrete on from above is easier than the hand labor of throwing the concrete up onto the roof surface to spread it out.

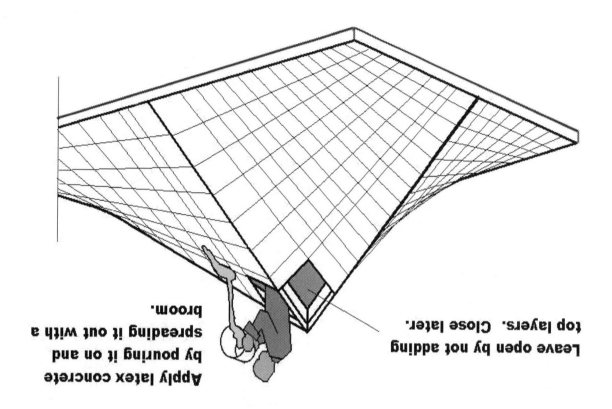

Apply latex concrete by pouring it on and spreading it out with a broom.

Leave open by not adding top layers. Close later.

Figure 9   Crown Access Hole for Applying Latex Concrete

Natural Ventilation

The above access hole can be left permanently open in the construction to serve as a smoke port, or roof ventilation hole. It is often advisable to provide for ventilation of thin concrete shells particularly in the summers in arid climates. Figures 10 and 11 give two alternative ways of providing crown ventilation.

Frame across between ridge beams and wrap fabric to attach to form crown openings.

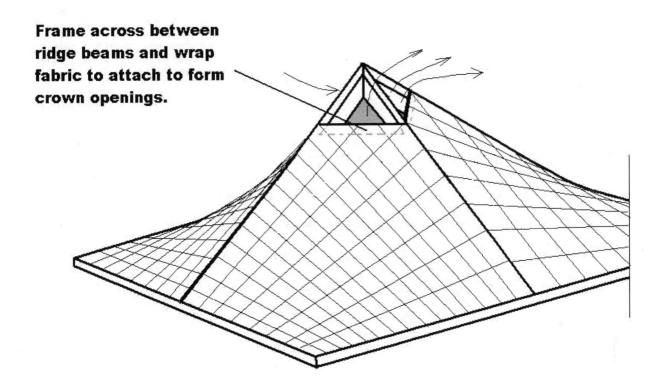

Figure 10   Crown Ventilation by Providing Edge Supported Fabric

Covering the vent in Figure 10 provides a rain hood as seen in Figure 11, and will likely reduce the nuisance of birds perching on the edge of the vent opening.

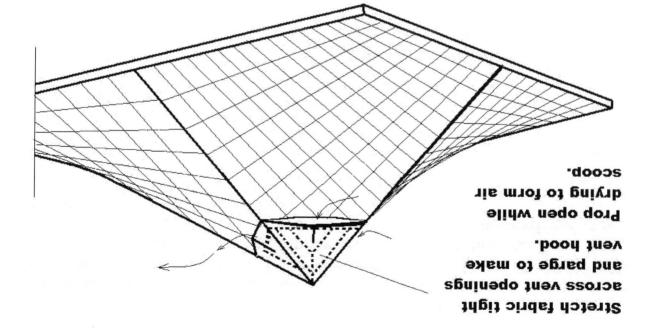

Figure 11 Crown Ventilation with Rain Hood

Stretch fabric tight across vent openings and parge to make vent hood.

Prop open while drying to form air scoop.

Strength and Attachment of Shells

Mathematics of Shells

Much of the mathematics of HP shells was presented in Chapter E. In that chapter equations for geometry, surface area and the central length or running diagonal length of a shell were derived. Methods were given to calculate loads and membrane stresses in the shells. Please refer to that chapter when these properties are desired.

Strength and Attachment of Shell Roof Surfaces

In this section we will discuss physical testing to prove the structural adequacy of an HP latex concrete shell roof.

In the photograph below, students at West High School in Denver, Colorado are seen loading the surface of a small HP shell using tubes filled with sand. The sand is seen stockpiled on the ground beyond the shell. Before loading was stopped, the students had piled 6 feet of sand onto the shell, and the shell exhibited no signs of distress. The bags were cut-open automobile inner-tubes filled with sand, then the ends were tied closed with wire. The tubes could be tied in place on the steep slopes of the shell to maintain a uniformly distributed weight on the shell. Six feet of sand was equivalent to about 20 feet of very wet snow. Thus great strength of the shell was demonstrated.

Figure 12, Students Testing a Shell Roof Model

In a similar fashion, the strength of large shells can be verified by overloading them by a factor of two (2.0) over what the shell might receive during its service life, and

(1) seeing that they do not collapse or show signs of distress, or

(2) noting that when the load is removed after the shell has been loaded for 24 hours, it rebounds to within 20 percent of its original location.

If the shell returns or nearly returns (within 20 percent) to its original undeformed shape, then the shell is considered to have passed a reasonable test for structural adequacy.

Testing for the Strength of Fabric

A second major concern over the strength of shells is the strength of the fiberglass fabric and the latex concrete surface made from it. We take a conservative approach. The latex concrete will have a tensile strength without the fabric. This can be an ultimate strength as high as 500 pounds per square inch of shell thickness. Thus a shell with a half-inch thick layer of latex concrete on it can have a failure strength of 200 to 250 pounds per running inch of cross section. However, because we will likely have supervision with little experience in this construction in remote areas in our fight against village poverty, and because we may have low concrete strength, or cracking of the concrete due to rapid drying, we will ignore this hidden strength. We will assume that *only the fabric* will be active in resistance to tensile load.

The fabric can be tested for its tensile strength by taking a strip of it and pulling it apart in tension. Testing for fabric strength was first discussed in Chapter D. Consider the fabric wrapped around blocks as shown in Figure 13 below. Four short pieces of 2x4 lumber are wrapped with a 2-inch wide strip of fabric attached as shown in the sketch. The outer heads of two of the blocks are rounded so that the tension in the fabric is spread uniformly by passing over a surface that develops frictional resistance against the fabric. Thus the fabric will tear apart in the span between the blocks, and not at the staples used to anchor the fabric to the back side of the blocks. The blocks are then pulled carefully apart until the fabric fails. The *unit* load in pounds per linear inch of width at failure of the 2-inch wide strip is its failure load divided by 2 inches, the wide of the strip. If the fabric tears apart at 400 pounds applied load, the strength of the fabric is 200 pounds per linear inch, or 2400 pounds per foot of width of fabric. Fiberglass fabric will be shown to be considerably stronger than other fabrics in common use.

We have had to measure the force applied to the fabric in the test above. If the tester has access to a tensile force gauge, so much the better for accuracy. However, often the tester is in a remote area and does not have access to an accurate scale. In that case, the tester has to improvise.

Consider the following method.

The 2-inch strip of fabric can be draped over any convenient horizontal support, and weights can be suspended from the strap. The simple frame in Figure 14 below allows the fabric to be wrapped over a convenience loading surface, possibly shaped like the blocks shown in 13.

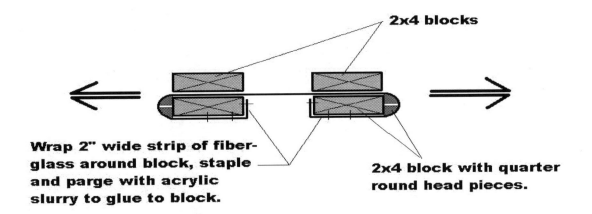

2x4 blocks

Wrap 2" wide strip of fiber-glass around block, staple and parge with acrylic slurry to glue to block.

2x4 block with quarter round head pieces.

Figure 13   Tensile Testing of Fabric

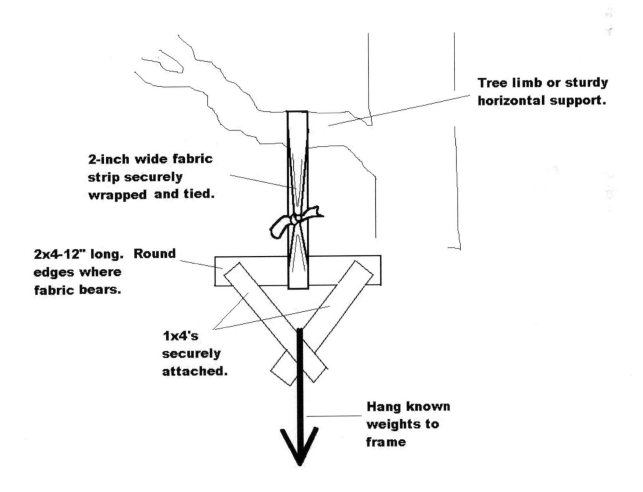

Tree limb or sturdy horizontal support.

2-inch wide fabric strip securely wrapped and tied.

2x4-12" long. Round edges where fabric bears.

1x4's securely attached.

Hang known weights to frame

Figure 14   Measuring the Strength by Hanging Weights

Known weights are then added until the strap breaks. For example, a large bucket can be suspended from the frame, and bricks of known weight are stacked into the bucket until failure occurs. The unit weight of a brick can be accurately determined by stacking ten bricks on a bathroom scale, and dividing the total weight by ten. Note that if 4 inches of fabric width are being used to carry the load, the strength of the fabric will be the failure load divided by 4, in pounds per linear inch of width of strap.

Attaching Shells to Columns

In the sketches of Figure 15 below are shown how shells can be attached to columns using latex slurry ties. The process is done in six steps. The sketches are self explanatory.

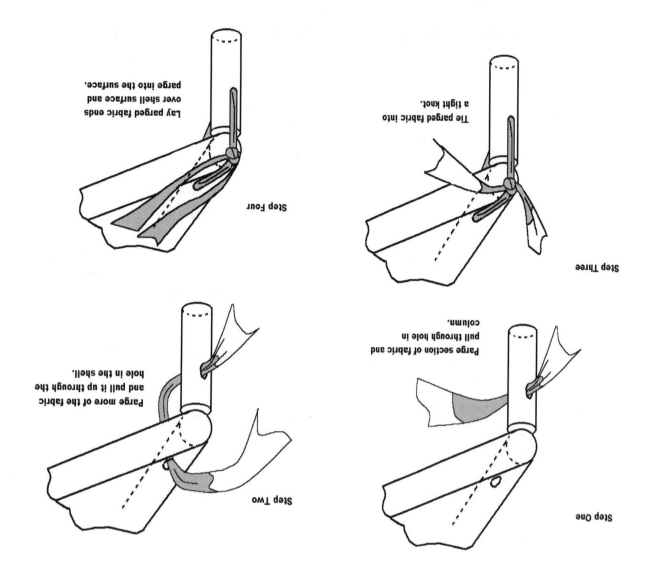

Step One

Parge section of fabric and pull through hole in column.

Step Two

Parge more of the fabric and pull it up through the hole in the shell.

Step Three

Tie parged fabric into a tight knot.

Step Four

Lay parged fabric ends over shell surface and parge into the surface.

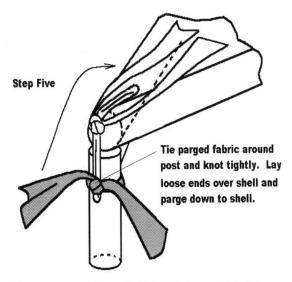

Step Five

Tie parged fabric around post and knot tightly. Lay loose ends over shell and parge down to shell.

Repeat this step three times to fully encapsulate tie down in parged fabric.

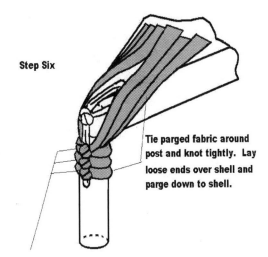

Step Six

Tie parged fabric around post and knot tightly. Lay loose ends over shell and parge down to shell.

Repeat this step three times to fully encapsulate tie down in parged fabric.

Figure 15 (Steps One through Six)

Wind Loading on Shell Surfaces

One of the questions not thoroughly covered in prior chapters was the response of shell surfaces to wind. A technique was presented to approximate the overturning loads on shells in order to determine the required strength of ties needed to anchor them down.

The actual force applied by a wind to the curvilinear shell will involve inward pressure on the near or windward walls, inward pressure on the windward roof surfaces applied perpendicular to the roof surfaces, suction or uplift pressure on the far roof surfaces applied perpendicular to those roof surfaces, and an outward horizontal pressure on the downstream or leeward walls. In addition, outward or suction pressures will be applied to the windward edges of the lateral wall surfaces caused by wind rounding the leading corners of those lateral walls.

It can be seen from the discussion of the West High School shell on pages 85-86 above that the strength of the shell itself to surface loading is quite high, and need not be of concern for wind loading. A technique for verifying the adequacy of columns and tie downs is discussed below.

Lateral Wind Loads on Columns

Lateral wind loads are resisted by columns and column tie down systems. The complex set of forces discussed above can be approximated for determining the required strengths of columns and tie downs by taking a projected area as shown in Figure 16 of say 30 feet wide by 10 feet tall times 20 pounds per square foot, the horizontal pressure

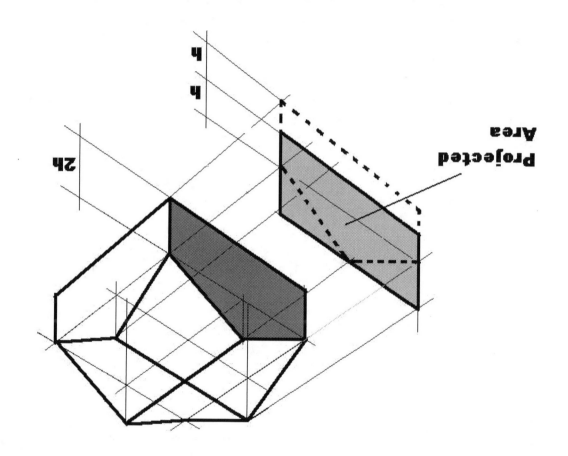

Figure 16   Projected Area of Wind Loaded Shell

that would be applied to a bill board of those dimensions by a 100 mph wind. The load would be an area of 30 x 10 or 300 square feet times 20 pounds per square foot or 30' x 10' x 20 psf = 6000 pounds of horizontal force. If the columns and tie downs can resist a force half again as much as this 6000 pound force (a factor of safety of 1.5), the structure is deemed capable of withstanding the 100 mph wind "with safety". That is a force at failure of 9000 pounds.

For the case of *roofs-only* **construction** this can be approximated by tightly stretching a rope between two column tops, and applying a load in the middle of the stretched rope by the technique shown in Figure 17 below.

Strength of Columns

Testing of Buried Anchors

The magnitude of the applied load for the above condition can be taken as 9000 pounds divided by the number of columns which will resist it, say for this shell, 4 columns. Therefore, the rope tension must be on the order of 9000 / 4 = 2250 pounds. The amount of sand to be placed in a tray suspended from the rope, and the angle of the rope to cause a 2250 pound rope tension, can be determined experimentally by applying the sand load in the center of a horizontally stretched rope, and measuring the dimensions and sag of the rope, then using the equation below where d and h are field measured.

$$T = W\,d\,/\,2\,h = 2250 \text{ pounds}$$

Therefore, $h\,/\,d = 4500\,/\,W$ = a known value.

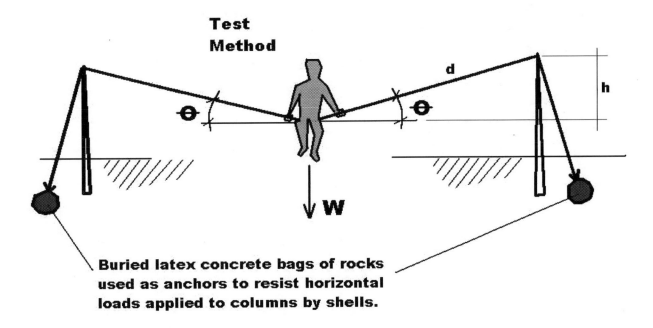

Figure 17 Testing for Tie Down Anchorage Strength

This method of applying tension in ropes is also discussed on page 94 under "Tensile Strength of Ropes."

In Figure 17 is illustrated the method of testing when tie down anchors are used to keep the columns vertical, and the column is assumed to carry little lateral load by itself. Note that the anchor will only resist load applied in the plane formed by the column and the anchor rope. If greater strength is required, use multiple tie downs at angles to each other as in Figure 18 on the next page.

Bending Strength of Columns

The required bending strength of columns can be approximated by taking the horizontally applied wind force on a shell, plus half the horizontally applied wind force on the walls as a combined horizontal load applied to the tops of the columns. This combined load tends to pull the columns over, causing each column to either break due to flexural overstress, or to rotate and pull out of the ground at its base due to inadequate anchorage in the soil. The magnitude of the bending moment at the base of the column (in foot-pounds) is the product of the applied force times the height of the column. The column itself must be strong enough to carry this moment in bending, and the anchorage of the column in the soil must be strong enough to not allow column rotation and pullout.

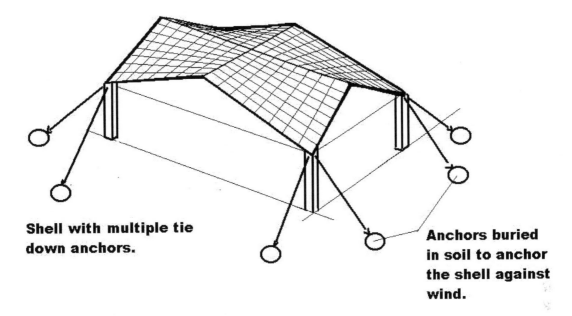

Shell with multiple tie down anchors.

Anchors buried in soil to anchor the shell against wind.

Figure 18   Multiple Tie Down Anchors

Testing for Required Column Strength

Earlier we calculated a laterally applied load of 2250 pounds applied a the top of he column by a 30'x30' shell. Therefore, if we test it and it can carry 2250 times a factor of safety of 1.5, or 3375 pounds, it will be deemed "safe" at 100 mph. 3375 pounds is about as much as a heavy pickup truck can pull in low gear on dry asphalt pavement.

The field worker can test his proposed column for adequate strength by tying a rope to the top of the pole and pulling on it with his pickup truck. If the pole breaks, use a larger one. If the pole pulls out of the ground, bury it deeper until the truck can neither break it or pull it out of the ground. Wrap the base of the column as shown in Figure 20 below.

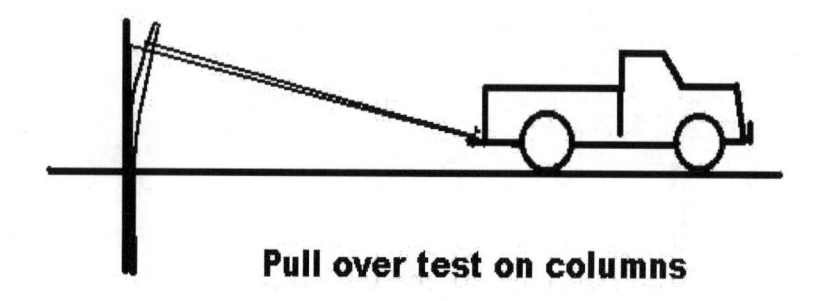

Pull over test on columns

Figure 19   Pull Test with Truck

Rot of Column Bases

The strength of columns in part depends of the protection of column bases from rot and insect attack. Shown in the sketches which follow are techniques for protecting column bases using latex concrete. Bamboo, willows or woody stems bound together with fabric and latex slurry can form a column. Bundles should be heavily parged to make their interior waterproof.

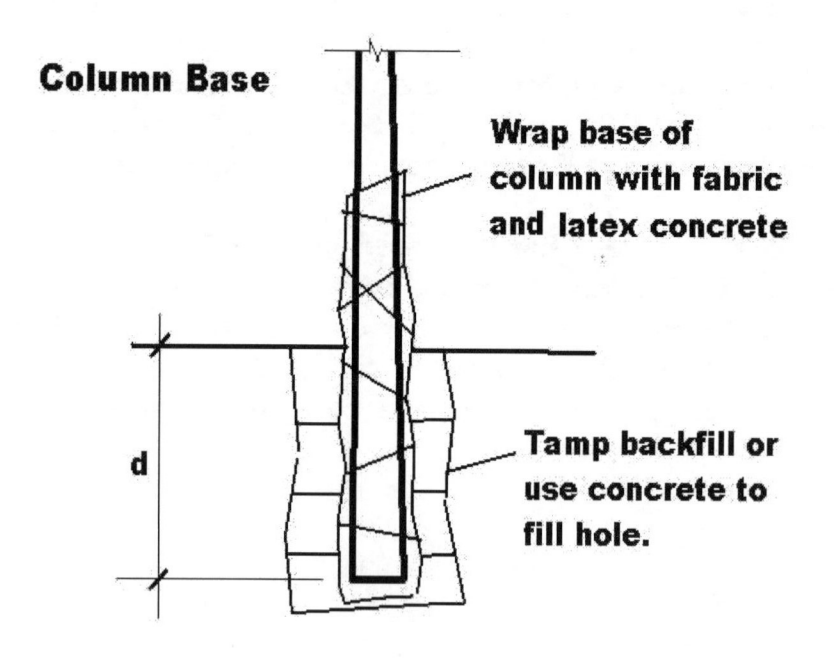

Figure 20   Protection of Base of Normal Column

Column or Pole Base

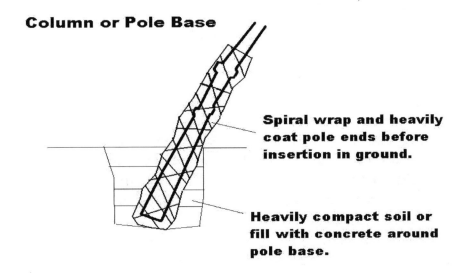

Spiral wrap and heavily
coat pole ends before
insertion in ground.

Heavily compact soil or
fill with concrete around
pole base.

Figure 21   Waterproof Cover on Pole Base

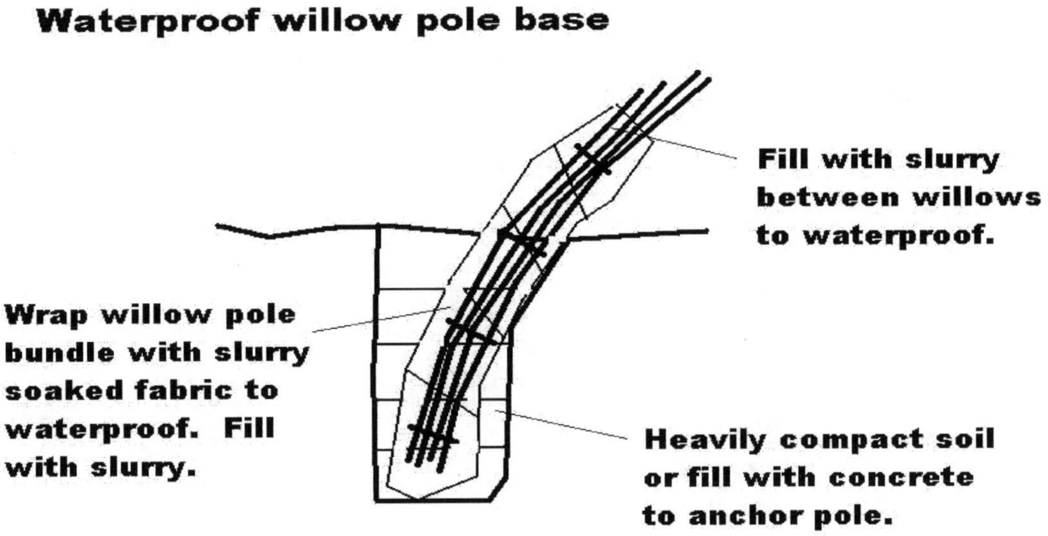

Waterproof willow pole base

Fill with slurry
between willows
to waterproof.

Wrap willow pole
bundle with slurry
soaked fabric to
waterproof. Fill
with slurry.

Heavily compact soil
or fill with concrete
to anchor pole.

Figure 22   Protection of Bases of Willow-Bundle Columns

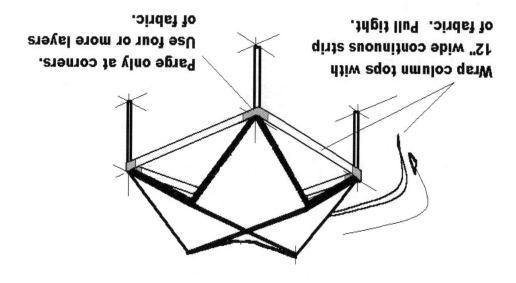

Ties for Shell Spread

Perimeter Ties for Shell Roofs:

Shell roofs which rest on their points as shown in Figure 8 on page 77 tend to spread under load. This spreading should be resisted by tension ties as shown in Figure 8, or by wrapping the perimeter of the shell at its column heads with a tension tie or rope of latex slurry impregnated fabric as shown below in Figures 23 and 24.

A strip of fabric 12 inches wide can be cut from a roll of the fabric, and spliced into a long strand by coating the fabric with latex slurry at the slices. The number of layers of fabric used in the tie should be selected to match the tensile strength of the tie required by structural analysis.

Tension Tie to Resist Spread

Wrap column tops with
12" wide continuous strip
of fabric. Pull tight.

Parge only at corners.
Use four or more layers
of fabric.

Figure 23   Perimeter Ties Being Installed

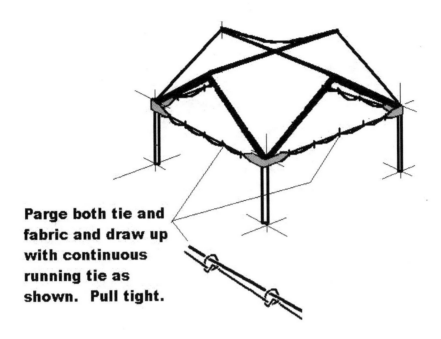

Parge both tie and fabric and draw up with continuous running tie as shown. Pull tight.

Figure 24   Perimeter Ties Completed

Cross Ties for Shell Roofs

The same shell can be braced against lateral spreading of the column tops by using ties which cross in the middle of the shell as shown in the figure below.

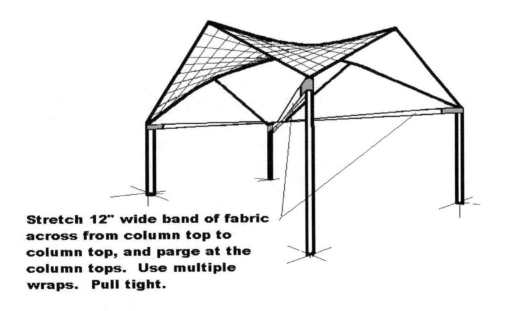

Stretch 12" wide band of fabric across from column top to column top, and parge at the column tops. Use multiple wraps. Pull tight.

Figure 25   Cross Ties for Shells Wrapped

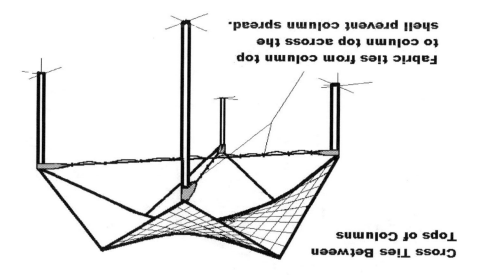

Cross Ties Between
Tops of Columns

Fabric ties from column top
to column top across the
shell prevent column spread.

Figure 26 Cross Ties for Shells Completed

As the ties are stretched across the shell to the opposite column top, the strip of fabric can be twisted 180 degrees to make the strips lie flat against each other at the center of the shell.

After the strips of fabric are stretched, the strips are bundled with a running tie as shown in the shell in Figure 24 above.

Tensile Strength of Ropes

A rope or tie can be made with latex slurry by taking a width of fabric, coating or soaking it in latex slurry, and twisting the fabric into a strand. When the soaked fabric hardens under tension, a coarse rope has been produced.   The strength of such a rope can be determined by using the technique illustrated in Figures 13 and 14 on page 83. The strength of a one-inch wide strip of fabric is determined, then the strength found is multiplied by the width in inches of the fabric used in making the twisted rope.

A technique for determination of the strength of a rope when you do not know the strength of the soaked fabric is to tie the rope between two trees or firm anchorage points, and sit in the the middle of the rope.

This method was first discussed for testing for strength of buried anchors on page 87 above. This discussion is extended as follows.

The rope will sag as shown in Figure 27 below. If you are sitting such that the rope makes the same angle theta on each side of you, and you have a friend take a picture of you, you can measure the angle from the photograph. You can also determine the angle theta by measuring distances d and h as shown on the force diagram. From these dimensions you can draw the force diagram on a sheet of paper, and do the following calculation:

The rope tension T is found by:

Sin theta = h / d,   and is measured from the photograph,

By similar triangles, T is to d as W is to 2h

Therefore, T = W d / 2h

We can also just draw the force diagram shown immediately below to a scale of say 1 inch equals 100 pounds, and measure the comparative lengths of W and T.

T will be proportional to W as the length of d on our drawing is to the length 2h.

If my weight W is 200 pounds, and the rope sag is 3 feet in a 20 foot run of rope (distance d), then the tension in the rope is

T = 200 (20) / 6 = 667 pounds.

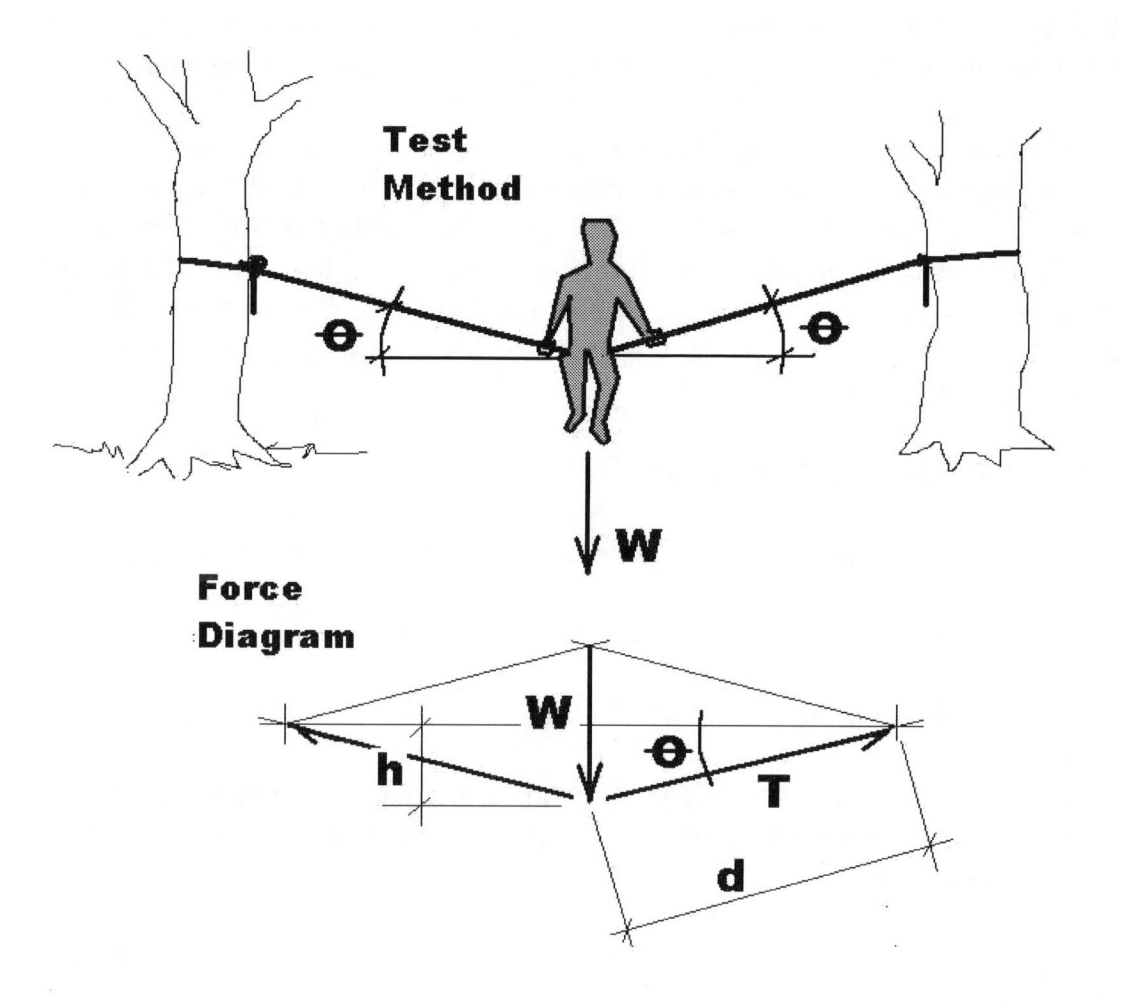

Figure 27   Measuring Rope Tension Experimentally

By this test, and assuming that the rope does not break, we know that the rope will carry at least **667** pounds.   The rope is at least that strong.

We can determine the precise ultimate strength of the rope by adding weight (say to a tray of sand bags of known weight) until the rope breaks, and knowing the weight under which it broke, plus the corresponding values of d and h by measurement, we can back-calculate the load at which the rope broke.

Insulating Shells

Light Weight Insulation

A thin latex concrete shell roof can make a dwelling cold in the winter and hot in the summer. In the winter, a half inch of concrete is not a significant barrier against outside temperature due to its thermal conductivity. In the summer the gray color absorbs heat, so the shell becomes a heat transmitter and radiator. It is advisable to insulate shells intended for habitation. If the shell has an attic floor, the floor can be loaded with insulative material.

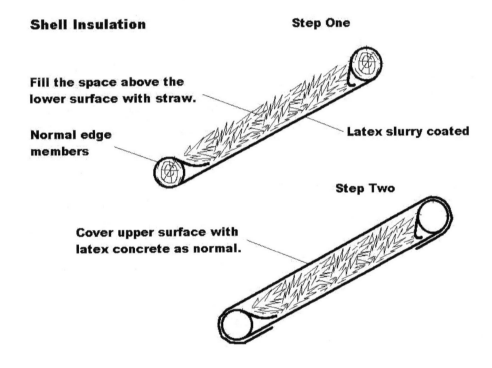

Shell Insulation

Fill the space above the lower surface with straw.

Normal edge members

Step One

Latex slurry coated

Step Two

Cover upper surface with latex concrete as normal.

Figure 28   Thermally Insulated Shells

But also, the shell itself can be made into a thermal blanket for the habitat. If on the bottom surface of the shell edge and ridge members a membrane is stretched, lightly parged with slurry and allowed to harden before the top surface is placed, the space between the surfaces can be filled with a variety of insulating materials such as straw, sewn in place blankets, shredded and treated (fireproofed) paper, or fiberglass batting, then the top surface can be added as usual, and heavily parged with latex concrete.

Insulating with Adobe

A construction which will provide warmth for a long period of time due to its heat capacity is the adobe insulated shell shown below. The adobe material (mud mixed with straw, then dried into bricks) once it warms up, will retain heat and provide greater winter comfort. But the material is also heavy, and sensitive to wetting. Therefore, the two shell surfaces should be strongly sewn together (laced through the dried mud blocks) so that the weight is being carried by the stronger upper shell, as well as the lower shell. The lower fabric surface can be lightly parged and left porous so that trapped moisture can escape. The top shell should be heavily parged and waterproof.

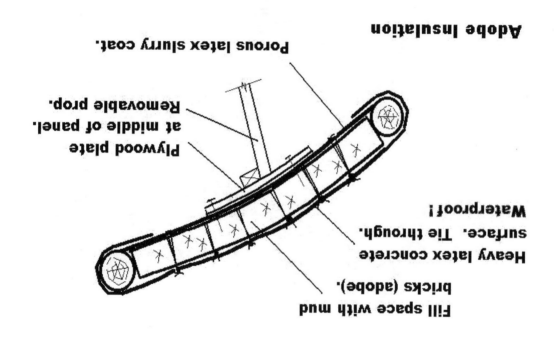

Fill space with mud bricks (adobe).

Heavy latex concrete surface. Tie through. Waterproof!

Plywood plate at middle of panel. Removable prop.

Porous latex slurry coat.

Adobe Insulation

Figure 29   Adobe-filled Shell Cavity

It is to be noted that the indigenous architecture of many near east nations is heavy mud and wattle roofs on heavy mud walls. This architecture is unsafe due to roof collapse from overloading as more mud is added during each annual repair. It is also dangerous because of its inherent structural weakness against earthquake. A suggestion is to use the light weight concrete shells without insulation supported over the existing mud roof construction to shed rain. It will greatly reduce the problems of maintenance inherent when mud construction is left exposed to weather.

Ideas for Arch Shell Construction

Arch Construction:

The HP shells discussed above have a fabric stretched tightly across between frame members, stapled down, and when parged with a liquid latex and Portland cement slurry, then allowed to harden into a stiff shell. The shell carries its load through in-plane stresses by shell action. Arched structures, such as the ones shown below, consist of fabric sewn or tied to arched members, but the fabric is not necessarily stretched tight before parging. The slurry hardens and sags and gives the arched covering its structural stiffness, but the ribs are the primary structural load carrying elements, not the shell surface itself.

Figure 30 Arched Shelter Habitat

Model by George Nez

The arched structure shown in Figure 31 can be fabricated to make a cover for a water storage lagoon. The outward thrust of the arches is carried in the horizontal ties which frame across the span of the arch at its base. These ties can be made of fabric, parged and twisted into rope. A group of workers can carry this shell around, and position it over a water supply.

Figure 31   Arched Lagoon Cover

Model by George Nez

Ideas for Water Collection and Storage

Latex Concrete Shells for Water Collection:

In the sketch below, construction of a well is depicted, followed by construction of a drainage basin which delivers water to the well during the rainy season. This water replenishes the ground water for use during the dry seasons. The replenishment of wells by surface water collection systems has been successfully used in India.

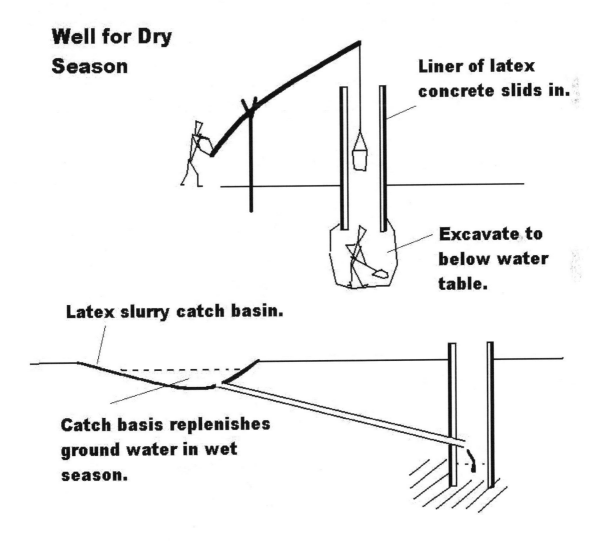

Well for Dry Season

Liner of latex concrete slids in.

Excavate to below water table.

Latex slurry catch basin.

Catch basis replenishes ground water in wet season.

Figure 32 Collection of Rainwater Runoff During the Wet Season

Schemes for Water Storage

Latex liquid can be mixed into soil and rolled out to make it flat. Roads have been built in the jungles of Venezuela using latex sludge, a by-product of the latex industry. The sludge is sprayed on and turned into the soil and hand or roller compacted. This same technique can be used to harden the floors of native huts, greatly increasing their resistance to boring insects, and provided an improvement in the health of the occupants.

Similarly, latex can be used to harden soil for making ponds and water catch basins. In the sketch shown in Figure 33 below, the floor is hardened, then either fiberglass fabric can be nailed down to it, or a mat of willows can be placed over the hardened soil, and fiberglass fabric can be tied to the mat. The fabric is then painted or filled with latex slurry. A hard shell for water containment can be made using final layers of latex concrete. When sufficiently filled with slurry and concrete, the mat can hold water.

It is recommended that several basins be built to work out the techniques of construction.

Stream Fed Water Storage Pond
or Catch Basin

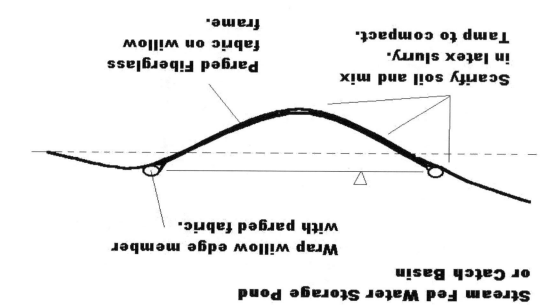

Wrap willow edge member
with parged fabric.

Parged Fiberglass
fabric on willow
frame.

Scarify soil and mix
in latex slurry.
Tamp to compact.

Figure 33   A Catch Basin or Pond for Storage of Water

Below is shown a permanent cover erected over a water catch basin. Willows are bound together to form ribs, and are bent to arch out over the basin. The bases of the ribs are wrapped with fabric and heavily parged with latex slurry to make them resistant to rot and insect attack.

The ribs are then tied together across the top of the cover, and horizontal willow rings are tied to the ribs. The resulting mat of willows is covered with fabric tied in place, then parged with latex slurry and concrete. The resulting surface can support the weight of workers and users of the basin.

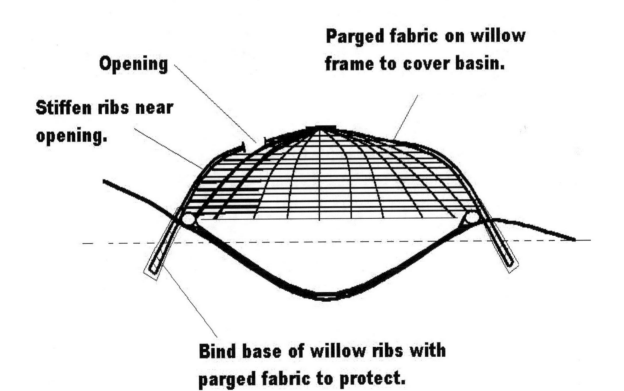

Willow Frame Cover for Water Supply

Parged fabric on willow frame to cover basin.

Opening

Stiffen ribs near opening.

Bind base of willow ribs with parged fabric to protect.

Figure 34   Permanent Cover for a Water Storage Pond

Rainstore³ A recent development in underground water storage tanks is an assembly of nested plastic forms spaced apart in a grid by plastic ties, the stacked assembly holding water by being wrapped in an impervious liner. These strong space racks are stacked four to eight feet high and wrapped with heavy sheet plastic. The nest then becomes the form upon which a ground surfacing can be placed. This surfacing can be a heavy concrete slab for parking trucks, porous pavers for surface water collection, or "*Grasspave²*" a turf reinforcement plastic form paving for grassland playgrounds. The volume of underground forms, *Rainstore³*, can be filled with water for use by the village as underground water storage. The *Rainstore³* products can be obtained by contacting *Invisible Structures, Inc.* 1597 Cole Blvd, Suite 310, Golden Colorado, 80401, USA.

Rain Water Collection Using Multiple Shells

Rain water can be collected on surfaces which drain to a collection point or basin. Often downspout water is collected into rain barrels, or is filtered and stored in underground containers such as Rainstore³, or is led to wells or drains which replenish the underground aquifers during the rainy season.

Shell roofs often cover large areas, and hence are natural surfaces for collecting rain water. Please refer to Figure 35 below.

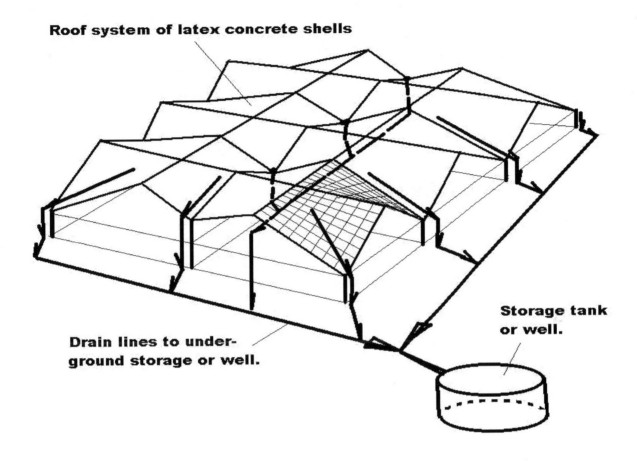

Roof system of latex concrete shells

**Drain lines to under-
ground storage or well.**

**Storage tank
or well.**

Figure 35   Collection of Rain Water for Underground Storage

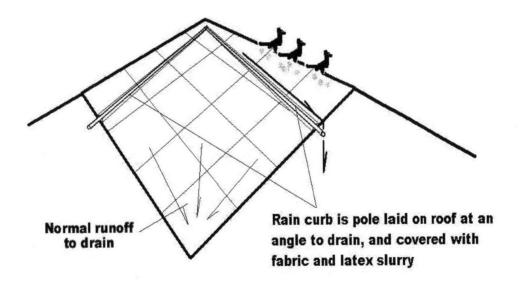

**Normal runoff
to drain**

**Rain curb is pole laid on roof at an
angle to drain, and covered with
fabric and latex slurry**

Figure 36   Curb to channel bird droppings off roof

A problem with rain water storage is that debris or bird droppings accumulate on the roof surface and are washed into the drinking water container. Figures 36 and 37 illustrate methods of preventing or lessening this problem.

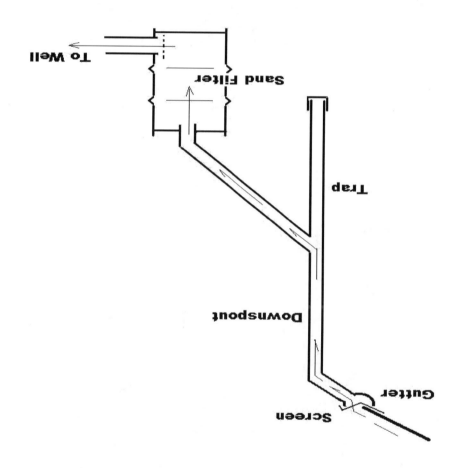

Figure 37   Filtering Rain Water for the Well

The components of the system, the gutter, the downspout piping, and the sand filter barrel can all be made from latex concrete by wrapping fabric around forms and applying the latex slurry. After the slurry has hardened, latex concrete can be added for strength and water tightness.

This type of downspout with plastic pipes and steel drum filters was developed by young engineers in India to help the villagers collect rain water on a village-wide scale.

Ideas for Waterless Toilets

A Sloped Tray Waterless Toilet

Many displaced people groups are eking out an existence in arid climates where water is at an absolute premium. It is certainly not available for flushing toilets. Therefore, human waste is often dumped on the ground and left. These arid regions need toilet facilities which do not depend on water in order to regain and maintain the health of the population. It is particularly important as an aspect of school construction.

The Sloping Tray Design shown in Figure 38 collects the waste materials on a sloping surface allowing the liquids to drain through the tray to be evaporated up the chimney, or carried away into a leach field. The solids are retained on the tray for composting and later use as field fertilizer.

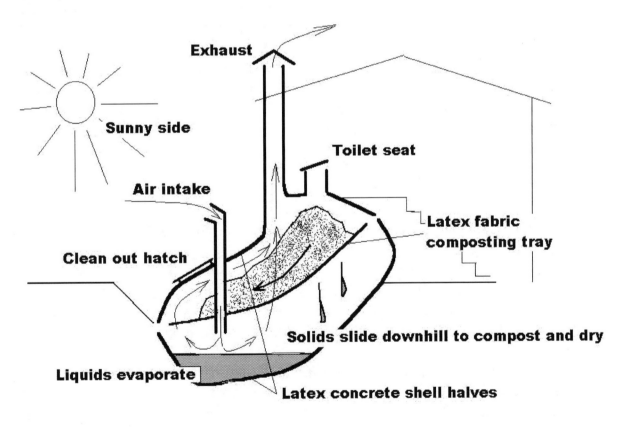

Figure 38   Waterless Toilet Concept

The sloping tray is a fiberglass screen using latex cement and slurry for construction. The upper and lower halves of the chamber are built separately and fitted together, half buried into the ground. The container is positioned on the sunny side of a building, or in the open, so that solar energy is absorbed and used to facilitate evaporation and air flow to the exhaust. The upper shell can be lifted off in its entirety for cleanout, or the cleanout hatch can be used to gain access to the upper composted solid materials chamber.

The trays are built by stretching fiberglass fabric over a willow frame, parging the edge frame heavily with latex concrete to make it stiff, but parging the fiberglass screen itself only in an intermittent pattern to glue the layers of fabric together, but to let the liquids pass through to collect below. For proper flow of hot air through the assembly and up the chimney, the assembly should be sited on a slope most exposed to the sun.

The composting solids must be allowed to compost in an aerobic reaction (oxygen rich), not in an anaerobic reaction (oxygen starved). Aerobic action allows the material to compost into clean, usable, safe fertilizer. This requires the controlled addition of straw or other composting material. Anaerobic action will cause the material to decay without properly composting and will smell bad. The toilet should be maintained under the guidance of a knowledgeable person able to control and maintain the aerobic reaction.

Double Chamber Toilet

Another form of waterless toilet, shown in Figure 39, is capable of serving larger populations. Each chamber has two compartments which are used alternately. One side is actively in use for a year, and the other side is sealed and left unused for that year so that full composting can occur. Then the composted material is removed, and the other side is closed up to allow its charge to compost.

After decomposition, the chamber is cleaned out and made ready for re-use, while the other full chamber is sealed from use to start its decomposition. The composting requires air circulation which is allowed by the open block walls. The toilet fixture itself is specially designed to separate the waste fluids from the waste solids by being two-chambered. The liquid waste is discharged into the liquid waste stack, and the solid wastes are discharged into the solid waste stack. A separate urinal can be provided to minimize liquid uptake. The floor of the chamber is also sloped to drain liquid wastes

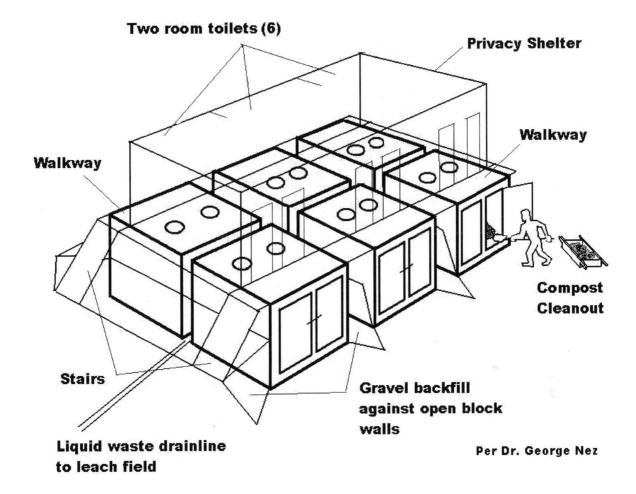

Figure 39   Double Chamber Waterless Toilets

In Figure 40 you can see that straw is used to line the chambers. Straw lines the chambers, and straw is added regularly though the soil stack during its use period to maintain the aerobic action of chemical decomposition. The volume of the waste material significantly decreases during aerobic decomposition.

Waste Cart Dry Toilet

A third concept that has many advantages is to use a wheeled plastic waste receptacle parked in the chamber below the toilet. Waste materials drop into the receptacle, and are caught on a screen suspended within the receptacle. The liquids drain through the screen and are piped to a leach field. The solids collect in the receptacle and when the receptacle is full, it is wheeled to a composting area away from the school or residence being serviced by the toilet.

Figure 40   Section Through Exterior Chamber

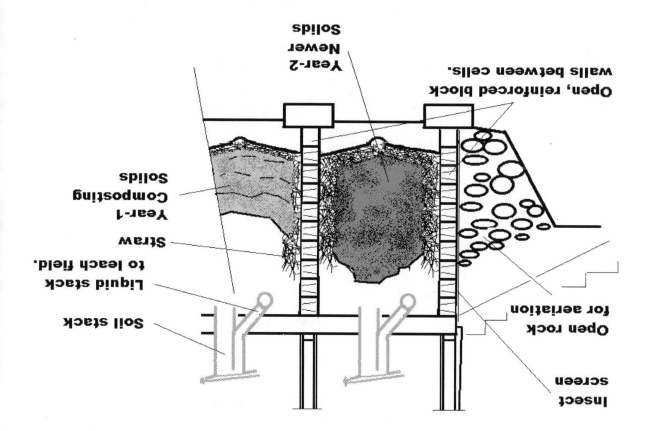

Year-2
Newer
Solids

Open, reinforced block
walls between cells.

Year-1
Composting
Solids

Straw

Liquid stack
to leach field.

Soil stack

Open rock
for aeration

Insect
screen

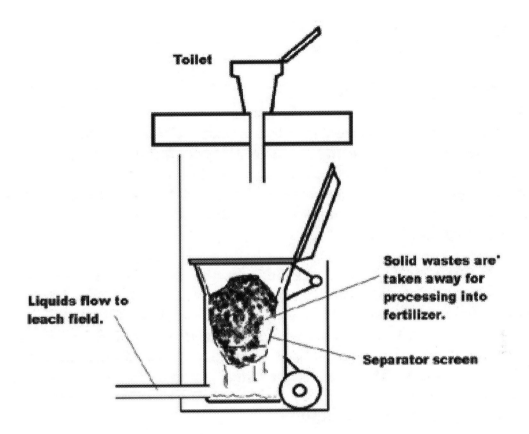

Figure 41 Waste Cart Dry Toilet

This system is receiving some acceptance in the rural United States in regions too new or too remote to have water-based sewer systems, or in communities which disallow on-site decomposition.

Ideas for Containers

A Grain Storage Container

Other uses for slurry treated fabrics can be found. In the sketch shown below a blanket of fabric several layers thick is laid on the floor to make a grain storage container. In the center of the fabric is poured a patch of latex concrete and allowed to spread out into a circular patch. This will be allowed to harden to become the floor of the grain storage container.

A mound of sand is then centered over the patch and the corners of the fabric are drawn up and tied together to form a lifting knot. A circular ring of willow reeds and latex slurry fashioned into a ring rope is inserted into the bag (or over the bag) and positioned on top of the mound of sand. The bag is then hoisted up and suspended from an overhead support. The sand causes the bag to assume the shape of a container as shown in Figure 41 below. The bag is left in contact with the floor to maintain a flat bottom.

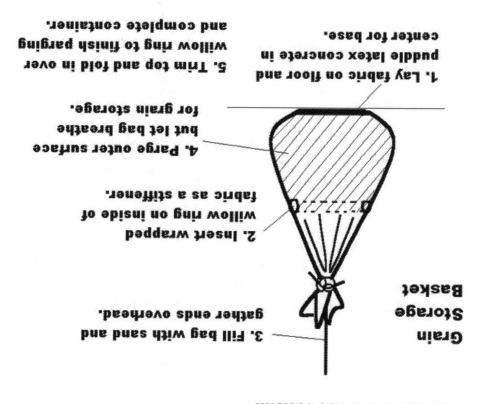

1. Lay fabric on floor and puddle latex concrete in center for base.

5. Trim top and fold in over willow ring to finish parging and complete container.

4. Parge outer surface but let bag breathe for grain storage.

2. Insert wrapped willow ring on inside of fabric as a stiffener.

3. Fill bag with sand and gather ends overhead.

Grain Storage Basket

Figure 41 Grain Storage Container

The portion of the bag at and below the level of the ring and sand can now be parged with latex slurry, but not so heavily that the slurry fills the holes in the fabric. The bag should be allowed to breathe as the grain later to be stored in it should be allowed to dry during storage to keep the grain from spoiling. Use just enough slurry to cause the bag to retain its shape when empty.

After the bag has hardened, the top can be trimmed down, the sand emptied out, and the top of the fabric can be turned into the bag and cemented in place, encapsulating the willow ring as an edge stiffener, and an attachment point for handles.

A Water Bucket   A second useful container can be fashioned out of fabric and latex slurry. The walls and base of a cylindrical bucket can be fashioned over a willow frame and sewn and cemented into shape.

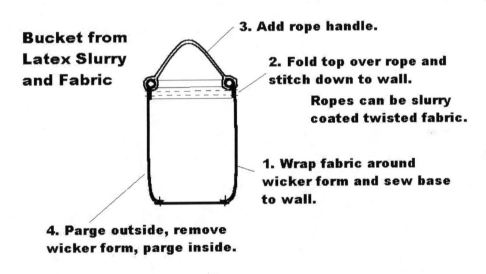

Bucket from Latex Slurry and Fabric

3. Add rope handle.

2. Fold top over rope and stitch down to wall.

Ropes can be slurry coated twisted fabric.

1. Wrap fabric around wicker form and sew base to wall.

4. Parge outside, remove wicker form, parge inside.

Figure 42   Water Bucket of Fabric and Latex Slurry

Further explanation of these concepts, and/or technical assistance on Latex Concrete Habitat may be obtained from:

Dr. George Nez   nezgeorge@gmail.com

The End

Appendix A

A School for Wardak Afghanistan Built by Dr. George Nez

Origins: Experimentation in earthquake reconstruction in Managua, Nicaragua in 1975 by Professor Joseph Kersavage and student volunteers from the University of Tennessee. The project was interrupted by civil war. Dr. George Nez brought it to the U.S. Park Service for further development, with engineering expertise from Dr. Albert Knott (Knott Testing Laboratory), and with latex cement chemistry assistance from Rohm and Haas Inc.

25-year-old and newer units, built in parks, camps, and recreation and research settings in various climates, remain in good condition.

First use in AFGHANISTAN was in 2003 in Wardak Province for a school. Three roof segments were built utilizing preexisting walls covered 1100 sq. ft. (110 sq. meters) to start the roofing of a 4000 sq. ft. building. See photograph below.

School in Wardak Afghanistan being built by Dr. George Nez.

Typical Features

Roof shell thickness – 7 mm to 1 cm.

Fiberglass screen is optimum reinforcement (but other fabrics are possible).

Form – double-arched hyperbolic paraboloid ("saddle shell")

Strength (live load plus dead load) readily 250 kg. per sq. meter (far above max. snow or wind loads).

Light weight – less than 20 kg. per sq. meter, far lighter than other roof systems. (Note: the traditional earth-covered roofs are 10 times heavier).

Earthquake resistance, being light and "un-twistable", little problem.

Roof ventilation and attic insulation can be built in.

Entire construction is done at ground level (no scaffolding or climbing).

Uses simplest hand tools, and common village labor.

Very economical: Total approximate cost per sq. meter:

Wood frame and ceiling	$ 10
Screen and staples	3
Cement and sand	1
Latex admixture	4
Transportation of materials and crane service	4
Labor	8
Total per sq. meter cost	$ 30

Durable: the latex admixture renders the concrete waterproof, resilient, and resistant to cracking.

Reparability: Large force penetration, like a tree limb falling, is readily repaired by cleaning out the fractured area, cementing new screen underneath, filling with latex cement, cementing fiberglass over the top and smoothing (repair practically invisible).

Chimney or other penetrations – readily opened in new thin cement surface by cutting and bending up the lips, inserting the stack, wrapping the lips against it with screen and re-cementing.

Fire resistance – nonflammable surface and frame members.

Savings elsewhere in the building – This roof is very light wall with corresponding savings in required wall and foundation strength. The stiff roof frame can span without loading the walls, or may be supported by the walls, or on it's own posts or columns, either built into the walls, or free standing. Very versatile.

Typical Construction Procedure

Calculate the tension stresses in the surface for a given size of roof panel to determine the number of screen layers needed.

Build frame at ground level: If adjacent to or exactly upon the building site, then a sizable roof like 6x6 meters can be built and raised.

If roofs need to be transported, they may be built in HALVES, for easy carrying, and erection at destination. Bolt or tie the half sections together.

Sections can be transported and erected when only the latex slurry coat is applied, before the latex concrete coats are added.

Screening: In several layers, overlapped, wrapped around edge and ridge members, stapled, then sealed with the first latex-cement slurry.

Cementing: First slurry coat of latex + portland cement + some water. Viscosity must be controlled to cause penetration through all fiberglass screen layers. Brush flat on both sides of surface to ensure full bonding with fiberglass. Cure for 24 hours.

After the latex slurry coat has cured, latex concrete coats may be added. Latex concrete is made by adding sand to the latex slurry. Sand can be added in increasing amounts in each layer. The first layer can be 1-part sand to 1-part cement, then 2-parts sand to 1-cement, then 3-sand to 1-cement and as always, limited water.

The final coat to seal the surface can be the original latex slurry. If final painting is desired, use only exterior grade latex paint "for concrete."

Always prewet the cured surface before adding the next layer, but sweep off any standing water.

Mix latex concrete in small batches (not by machine). It sets up quickly and must be brushed on immediately.

Joining roof units together: Bolt wooden edge frames together or bind together with twisted and latex-cement-soaked fiberglass rope. Lay fresh screen and cement across joints to seal. Slope the new valleys to outside drainage.

Re-roofing over old or damaged walls: Readily possible if wall tops are repaired to receive new roofs. Wall sections need not align with the roof edge frames if the frames have integral ceiling joists extending beyond the walls.

Roofs may be mounted on separate columns within or exterior to the walls, by placing columns at frame joints.

Roofs may be anchored over existing walls by cables extending down into foundation concrete, or to tied, parged and buried anchorage bundles.

Advice on Starting: Supervisors should first build one or more models of increasing size, to learn to handle the construction variables. Local laborers of modest skill can then be used.

End of Appendix A

Appendix B   Length of a Parabolic Arch

The running length of a parabolic arch is given by the equation[14]:

$$S = L \left[1 + \tfrac{2}{3} (2d/L)^2 - \tfrac{2}{5} (2d/L)^4 + \dots \right]$$ **Eq-B1**

where d and L are defined in the sketch below.

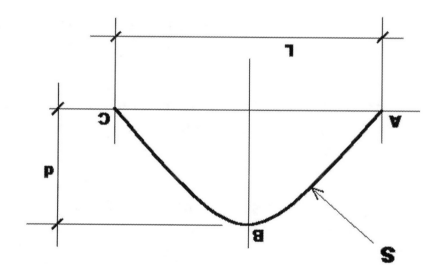

Figure B-1   Simple Parabolic Arch

It is noted that in the case presented in Chapter D on the 10x10x4 HP AC shell,[15] the arch shape, as given in Figure 4 of that chapter, is the same as the arch BC in the above diagram. In this case the length L in the above equation for S is twice the diagonal of the shell, and the resulting value of S will be halved to obtain just BC.

$$L = 2 \sqrt{(a^2 + b^2)}$$

$$d = h \quad \text{and}$$

$$2d/L = 2h / (2 \sqrt{(a^2 + b^2)}) \;=\; h / \sqrt{(a^2 + b^2)}$$

[14] Hudson, R.G., *The Engineers' Manual*, 2nd Edition, 1961, John Wiley & Sons, New York.

[15] Knott, A.W.: *Stress Analysis of an AC HP Shell Roof*, Proceedings, Sustainable Resources 2003 World Conference, University of Colorado College of Engineering and Applied Science, Boulder, Colorado, September 29 - October 4, 2003.

Therefore,

$$2S = 2\sqrt{(a^2 + b^2)}\left[1 + \tfrac{2}{3}\left(h/\sqrt{(a^2 + b^2)}\right)^2 - \tfrac{2}{5}\left(h/\sqrt{(a^2 + b^2)}\right)^4 + \ldots\right]$$

$$S = \sqrt{(a^2 + b^2)}\left[1 + \tfrac{2}{3}\left(h^2/(a^2 + b^2)\right) - \tfrac{2}{5}\left(h^4/(a^2 + b^2)^2\right) + \ldots\right] \quad \textbf{Eq-B2}$$

For the LC HP shell, which is 10' x 10' x 4' :

$$S = \sqrt{200}\left[1 + \tfrac{2}{3}(16/200) - \tfrac{2}{5}(256)/(200 \times 200)\right]$$

$$= 14.14\,(1 + 0.0533 + 0.0026) = 14.14\,(1.0559)$$

$$= 14.93 \text{ feet.}$$

Note that as the shell is relatively flat, the length of the parabolic arch is not much different from the length of the diagonal, $\sqrt{(a^2 + b^2)}$ = 14.14 feet.   The length, S, rather than $\sqrt{(a^2 + b^2)}$ should be taken as the correct arch length for most shells because it is used in determining the weight the shell must carry.

A Close Approximation

An approximation for shell arch length is to average the distances OgA and OA.   Note that the arch length is bounded by these two lines.

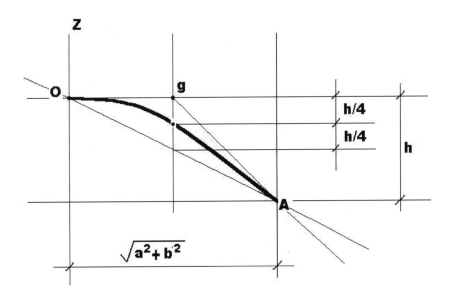

Figure B -2   The Geometry of the Shell Diagonal Midline OA

$$S = 0.5 \ (\ Og + gA + OA \ ) \qquad\qquad \text{Eq-B3}$$

$$\text{where } \ Og = 0.5 \sqrt{(a^2 + b^2)}$$

$$gA = \sqrt{(0.5 \sqrt{(a^2 + b^2)} \ )^2 + h^2} \ = \ 0.5 \sqrt{a^2 + b^2 + 4h^2}$$

$$OA = \sqrt{a^2 + b^2 + h^2}$$

Considering the 10x10x4 HP AC shell, these dimensions become:

$$Og = 0.5 \sqrt{(a^2 + b^2)} = 0.5 \sqrt{(200)} = 7.071'$$

$$gA = 0.5\sqrt{a^2 + b^2 + 4h^2} = 0.5\sqrt{100 + 100 + 64} = 0.5\sqrt{264} = 8.124'$$

$$OA = \sqrt{a^2 + b^2 + h^2} = \sqrt{216} = 14.697'$$

$$S = 0.5(Og + gA + OA) = 0.5(7.071 + 8.124 + 14.697') = 14.95 \text{ feet.}$$

For this shell, the two procedures give nearly identical results.

End of Appendix B

Appendix C   Surface Area of an HP Shell

The area of an HP shell is needed to determine the total weight of the shell. A common approximation is Area = ab where a and b are the plan dimensions of the HP shell. The true area of an HP shell is not an easy calculation to make. The following describes the process.

Consider the shell shown in Figure C-1 below.

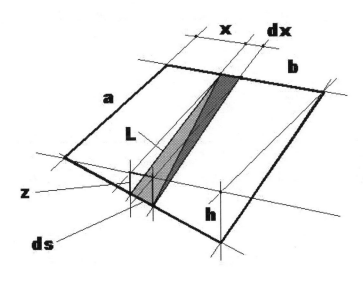

Plan Area = ab

Figure C-1 - Elements for Calculation of Shell Area

The surface area of a relatively steep shell is:

$$\text{Area} = \int_{o}^{b} dA = \int_{o}^{b} \tfrac{1}{2}\,(L\,dx + L\,ds) \qquad \text{Eq-C1}$$

$$\text{where} \quad L = \sqrt{(a^2 + z^2)}$$

$$z = xh/b \quad \text{and}$$

$$ds = dx\,\sqrt{(b^2+h^2)}\,/\,b$$

also[16] $\int \sqrt{(px^2+q)}\ dx\ =\ (x/2)\ [\sqrt{(px^2+q)} + (q/(2\sqrt{p}))\ \ln\ [\ x\sqrt{p}\ +\ \sqrt{(px^2+q)}\ ]$

Introducing the variables, and simplifying the equation, we obtain:

Area = $[(b+\sqrt{b^2+h^2})/4]\ [\sqrt{b^2+h^2}+(a^2/h)\ (\ln\ (bh+b\sqrt{a^2+h^2})\ -\ \ln\ (ab))]$ Eq-C2

For a shell that is 12 feet by 12 feet in plan, and 8 feet in rise, that would be:

Area $=\ [(12+\sqrt{208})/4]\ [\sqrt{208}+(144/8)\ (\ln\ (96+12\sqrt{208})\ -\ \ln\ (144))\ ]$

   $=\ [\ 6.6056\ ]\ [\ 14.422\ +\ (18)\ (\ \ln\ 269.067\ -\ \ln\ 144\ )\ ]$

   $=\ 95.266\ +\ 6.6056(18((5.5947)\ +\ 0.067(0.0037)\ -\ 4.9698)$

   $=\ 169.6\ $ sq. feet

which is 18 percent larger than the plan area, ab, of 144 square feet.

So, approximating the area as ab = 144 under-estimates the true area and the true shell weight by approximately 18 percent for a 12 x 12 x 8 shell.   It would under-estimate the area and weight of a 10 x 10 x 4 shell by 6 percent.

We can use one or the other of these two equations for Area in solving for the forces in the edge and ridge members, depending on the rise of the shell.

End of Appendix C

---

[16] Hudson, R.G., *The Engineers' Manual,* 2nd Edition, 1961, John Wiley & Sons, New York.

Notes-1

Notes-2

Notes-3

Notes-4

Printed in the United States
By Bookmasters